VICTORIAN CRITICAL INTERVENTIONS
Donald E. Hall, Series Editor

The AFFECTIVE LIFE *of the* AVERAGE MAN

The Victorian Novel and the Stock-Market Graph

❖

Audrey Jaffe

THE OHIO STATE UNIVERSITY PRESS

Columbus

Library of Congress Cataloging-in-Publication Data
Jaffe, Audrey.
  The affective life of the average man : the Victorian novel and the stock-market graph /
Audrey Jaffe.
      p. cm. — (Victorian critical interventions)
  Includes bibliographical references and index.
  ISBN-13: 978-0-8142-5171-3 (pbk. : alk. paper)
  ISBN-10: 0-8142-5171-4 (pbk. : alk. paper)
  ISBN-13: 978-0-8142-1115-1 (cloth : alk. paper)
  ISBN-10: 0-8142-1115-1 (cloth : alk. paper)
  [etc.]
  1. English literature—19th century—History and criticism—Theory, etc. 2. Stereotypes
(Social psychology) in literature. 3. Literature and society—England—History—19th
century. 4. Happiness in literature. 5. Money in literature. I. Title. II. Series: Victorian
critical interventions.
  PR468.S75J34 2010
  823'.809353—dc22
                                    2009029239

This book is available in the following editions:
Cloth (ISBN 978-0-8142-1115-1)
Paper (ISBN 978-0-8142-5171-3)
CD-ROM (ISBN 978-0-8142-9213-6)

Cover design by Janna Thompson-Chordas
Type set in Adobe Palatino
Printed by Thomson-Shore, Inc.

♾ The paper used in this publication meets the minimum requirements of the American
National Standard for Information Sciences—Permanence of Paper for Printed Library
Materials. ANSI Z39.48–1992.

9 8 7 6 5 4 3 2 1

CONTENTS

List of Illustrations • VII

Acknowledgments • IX

INTRODUCTION • 1

CHAPTER 1
Middlemarch: The Affective Life of the Average Man • 23

CHAPTER 2
Cardiac Excitability: Impulse, Restraint, and
"the Pulse of the People" • 42

CHAPTER 3
Trollope in the Stock Market: Irrational Exuberance
and *The Prime Minister* • 63

CHAPTER 4
David Copperfield's Happiness Economics • 81

CONCLUSION
Distant Reading • 102

Notes • 115
Works Cited • 129
Index • 135

ILLUSTRATIONS

Figure 1

Jevons's emotional intensity graph. From W. S. Jevons,
A Theory of Political Economy • 37

Figure 2

Cover by Raymond Meier, *New York Times Magazine,*
November 11, 2001 • 61

Figure 3

The stock market as seen through the body. From
Andrew W. Lo and Dmitry Repin, "The Psychophysiology of
Real-Time Financial Risk Processing," *Journal of Cognitive
Neuroscience* 14 (2002): 335 • 62

Figure 4

Ticker Man. Courtesy CNBC • 64

ACKNOWLEDGMENTS

For bearing with my graph obsession during the collapsed-bubble to collapsed-bubble period in which this book was written; for their willingness to listen, read, and advise; and for a truly unquantifiable amount of moral support, I am deeply indebted to Peter Schwartz, Mary Ann O'Farrell, Deborah Dyson, Emily Heady, Cathy Shuman, David Riede, and Jill Matus. For inviting me to address the "Victorian Business" Conference in 2002 and thus frightening me into writing my second chapter, I thank Joe Childers; the same thanks goes to the Tudor-Stuart Society of Johns Hopkins, whose invitation spurred my thinking about Trollope. Readers for *Victorian Studies* as well as Nancy Henry and Cannon Schmitt, in their capacity as editors of *Victorian Investments*, offered valuable comments on the Trollope chapter, and Indiana University Press has kindly allowed me to reprint it. Audiences at Indiana, the University of Toronto, McMaster, and the University of Waterloo were also gracious and helpful, as was a NAVSA seminar organized by Jill Matus. For directing me towards Canguilhem, my thanks to Dominique Colas. Raymond Meier has generously allowed me to reproduce his stunning *New York Times Magazine* cover of November 16, 2001; the MIT Press allowed me to reproduce the illustration that appears in chapter 2, and I thank CNBC once again for the use of their ticker-man. Thanks to Eli Schwartz for brainstorming about titles and for tech support at crucial moments, and to Peter Schwartz for everything.

INTRODUCTION

In 1889, Francis Galton wrote the following about the graph produced by what statistics calls the "law of error":

> *Order in Apparent Chaos.*—I know of scarcely anything so apt to impress the imagination as the wonderful form of cosmic order expressed by the "Law of Frequency of Error." . . . It reigns with serenity and in complete self effacement amidst the wildest confusion. The huger the mob, the greater the apparent anarchy, the more perfect is its sway. . . . Whenever a large sample of chaotic elements are taken in hand and marshalled in the order of their magnitude, an unsuspected and most beautiful form of regularity proves to have been latent all along. The tops of the marshalled row form a flowing curve of invariable proportions; and each element, as it is sorted into place, finds, as it were, a pre-ordained niche, accurately adapted to fit it. (66)

Galton's reverie expresses pleasure in the order and arrangement of a hitherto unorganized mass: the shape of the curve and the "invariable" proportions in which it flows. Anarchic elements are taken in hand and marshaled into a row—marshaled, indeed, into an "unsuspected" form of regularity discovered to have been present all along. But who or what is being marshaled? Galton's explicit reference is to the manipulation of points on a grid. It is not difficult, however, to see in his personifying trope, as well as in his references to the anarchic mob, the tops to which he refers not as points but rather as the tops of heads, and the elements being marshaled literally—as they are figuratively—as people. Galton's language suggests that the flowing curve exists in his imagination as a line of bodies, his statistical vision conflating the figure of the graph with those the graph is intended to represent. This interpretation is in keeping with his life's work, which was dedicated to the possibility of constructing, through an understanding of the mechanisms of inheritance, a more beautiful—because more orderly—population.[1] But the passage is striking not only because of its seamless substitution of bodies for points, but also because of Galton's evident pleasure and relief in the pattern he has discovered. The mapping of mathematical symmetry onto unruly elements appears as the solution to a social problem, transforming anarchy into beautiful form, wild confusion into a flowing curve.

Galton's was, of course, only one of many nineteenth-century attempts to devise coherent representations of the social whole. While Darwin worked to classify natural formations, animal species, and human populations, emerging social sciences such as anthropology and sociology sorted individuals and populations into categories of nation, race, class and gender. From the 1830s onward, the developing field of statistics used numbers, tables, and graphs with increasing frequency to enumerate and map selected aspects of selected populations. And in another register but similarly gesturing toward coherence, the period's preeminent literary form—the Victorian novel—relied for its political, ideological, and affective power on the existence of relationships it both presumed and constructed (and often constructed by presuming) between character and social formations: class, gender, nationality, and religion. Such classifications consolidate numerous distinct elements within single categories, in doing so creating new social objects and new objects of identification.[2] In general, what Mary Poovey has called "the imposition of a conceptual grid that enables every phenomenon to be compared, differentiated, and measured by the same yardstick" (*Social Body* 31) became, in the nineteenth century, not just a dominant practice in specific disciplines but a mode of perception, applied in widely varying areas of cultural discourse to disparate kinds of information.

The Affective Life of the Average Man is about the way representations of collective emotion shape perceptions of individual emotion and identity. It takes as its subject specific representations projected by the conceptual grid that takes literal form in, but is not limited to, the figure of the graph. And it draws on, and was indeed inspired by, the way representations of the stock market have, from the time of the market's early-Victorian popularization to the present day, served as a dominant means of assessing collective feeling: the graph, and other forms of stock-market rhetoric, tend to be viewed as reflections of feelings that, I argue, they both create and project.[3]

The cohesive images discussed here—the idea of the average man; the rhetorical construction of the stock market as a representation of emotion and character, and the use of "happiness" as a unifying term—come together in the stock-market graph and in other forms of stock-market rhetoric. These representations function in Victorian novels and cultural discourse not only as imagined consolidations of the social whole, but also as invitations to identification, constructing individual identity as the effect of an internalization of—and differentiation from—some synthetic representation of a group. Considered separately, as in my discussions of *Middlemarch* and *David Copperfield*, they construct characters as both viewers and viewed, their identities and emotions structured and mediated by representations of a larger cohesive whole. Considered together—as they are in the discussions of stock-market rhetoric and in the image of the stock-market graph at the book's center—they form a network of currencies of identity that overlap in surprising and suggestive ways, inviting new readings of Victorian culture, the Victorian novel, and the stock-market graph. The last in particular has not yet, to my knowledge, been sufficiently read at all, leaving unacknowledged and undiscussed both its widely-accepted status as a reflection of collective feeling and the assumptions about the relation between money and the emotions on which that status depends. The market, the graph, the novel; the idea of happiness and of the average man: all these phenomena project an image of the self as fundamentally vicarious; the effect of an encounter with external representations.

THIS BOOK is situated at the intersection of several areas of scholarship in Victorian literary and cultural studies. It shares with Nancy Armstrong's work on realism and photography, discussed in more detail below, the conviction that representations shape the realities they seem merely to represent. Mary Poovey's discussion of the production of abstract space in modern industrial capitalism in *Making a Social Body*, especially her conception of social organization produced on the model of a "schema or grid," emphasizes, as I do here, the nineteenth-century construction of the "social body" as an abstract form (29). Catherine Gallagher's work on economics and the body articulates in detail the idea, explored here as well, that the stories Victorian political economists tell about bodies and emotions are also told by Victorian novels. While I share with these critics an interest in the cohesive images of the social whole fashioned by Victorian institutions and modes of representation, my emphasis, however, is on the way novels and other forms of cultural discourse articulate interiority as an identification with particular representations. Conceptual grids devised to organize identities and emotions are, in the novels and cultural narratives I discuss, echoed in, and represented as manifestations of, the felt reality—the affective lives—of characters. Thus also relevant to this argument, though with an emphasis on a different kind of group representation, are readings at the intersection of economics and literary form by Deidre Lynch and Adela Pinch that describe eighteenth-century interiorities as the function of quotation, the inner lives of characters as a social space. In eighteenth-century studies as well, Terry Castle's attention to the shaping effects of such devices as thermometers and barometers reinforces my sense of the way dominant cultural narratives about quantification and measurement transform perceptions of interiority.

I rely throughout the book on Alain Desrosières's discussion of the political uses of statistics, especially his definition of the real as "a ground for action" (64). Similarly, I find enormously useful here, as I have in my previous work, Jacques Rancière's formulation of ideology as social consensus, which I draw from Kaja Silverman's discussion of gender ideology in *Male Subjectivity at the Margins*. Writes Silverman, "Like popular-democratic interpellation, the dominant fiction represents primarily a category for theorizing hegemony, and once again it functions as a mirror. Rancière defines it as 'the privileged mode of representation by which the image of the social consensus is offered to the members of a social formation and within which they are asked to identify themselves.'" This formation includes "the images and stories through which a society figures consensus; images and stories which cinema, fiction, popular culture, and other forms of mass representation presumably both draw upon and help to shape" (17). While Silverman and Rancière are chiefly concerned with the dominant fiction of family, the structures I discuss here shape social realities in a similar way. For despite influential dismantlings of the authoritative structures of Victorian science and economics, including work done under the rubric of the new economic criticism aimed at exposing the fictional status of economic terms, what appears as scientific authority in the form of numbers, graphs, and/or narratives about, for instance, the causes of economic crises continues to wield enormous cultural power and to compel individual and collective belief.[4] And belief, at both individual and collective levels, is crucial to the operation of ideology as Silverman, Rancière, and Desrosières describe it. As Silverman writes, "Ideological belief . . . occurs at the moment when an image which the subject consciously knows to be culturally fabricated nevertheless succeeds in being recognized or acknowledged as 'a pure, naked, perception of reality.'"[5] We may believe that scientific narratives or economic structures are fictional, that is, and at the same time behave as if they are true, making use of them, in Desrosières's terms, as a ground for action. Thus while part of this book's purpose is to account for the stock market's persistent imaginative hold—its ability to capture us by seeming to mirror us—it does so by addressing the larger representational structures that underwrite the market's rhetorical persuasiveness, in the form of the emotional coherence its quantifying, consolidating terms seem to offer our unruly identities.

"[M]odern abstraction," writes Poovey, "produces some phenomena as normative—ostensibly because they are more numerous, because they represent an average, or because they constitute an ideal towards which all other phenomena move. . . . " It "tends to be susceptible to the process of vivification that nineteenth-century writers like Marx and Freud referred to variously as reification, commodification, and fetishization" (*Social Body* 9). This book is centrally concerned with the vivification of modern abstractions, especially the kind that assimilate disparate phenomena to a single template or series of templates. It does not insist that these structures are primarily economic, though I share with Poovey, Gallagher, and others a recognition of that register's importance as an explanatory system from the nineteenth century to the twenty-first. But even as my argument acknowledges the privileged status of economic metaphors during this period, it is more concerned with quantification's general capacity to create currencies by collapsing differences, rendering the unreadable readable, giving form to what may otherwise be perceived as threateningly disorganized. Rather than break down abstractions to reveal the fractured realities they conceal (the goal, for instance, of Poovey's *Social Body*), I am interested in the way these cohesive images themselves not only become social realities, but structure representations of internal or psychological realities as well. This book explores the pervasive, generally unacknowledged presence of these images; their narrative exchangeability; and, in particular, representations of their internalization.[6] Just as Galton's "curve of invariable proportions" becomes a composite image, suggesting both a single, perfect individual and the mapping of an ideal form onto an entire population, so too do the representations discussed here function as templates or reference points for constructions of individual identity.

Though this project has affinities with critical work tying Victorian fiction to political economics, then, it is not a book about Victorian finance.

Similarly, while I discuss the historical foundation of the idea of the average in statistical theory and the history of the stock exchange, I am less concerned with actual mathematical averages and the presence of actual graphs than with the ways in which the ideas to which both give rise become evidence for the "reality" of cultural representations. In the readings offered here, the average man, the stock exchange or stock market, and the term "happiness," considered separately and, in the image of the stock-market graph, as they coalesce in a single figure, emerge as consolidations of multiple, never-completely knowable motivations and desires.[7] Like "race" and "gender"—composite terms that summarize realities too complex to be encompassed by single words—these names and categories function as currencies of identity, rendering dissimilar elements fungible and diverse individuals comparable. Attending to these structures, the readings offered here seek to challenge the way in which the idea of the average; the assumption that the market reflects a collective emotional life; and the consensus evoked by representations of specific emotions circulate in ordinary discourse as objective values.

This argument has implications for Victorian novel readers as well. The Victorian novel takes shape in a relation of mutual influence with emerging sociological and mass-cultural representations of the group; as Gallagher argues (in terms similar to Poovey's), novels often seem to vivify political economy's more abstract formulations (6). But even as Victorian novels draw upon and reflect the influence of political economy, so too do economic representations—in the form, for instance, of rhetoric about the stock market and the characters who participate in it—provide novelistic structures of narrative and character with a real-world context, at the same time inviting, as novelistic structures do so well, emotional investment: a felt identification with, and apprehension of the self's implication in, a coherent system of vivified abstractions. Carolyn Williams has written that, "in novelistic realism, the character's individuality is foregrounded but is always set against the aura of the social type" (116). But in the structure of identification on which Victorian novels tend to rely, neither representations of social types nor generalized representations of emotion remain "outside" the individual, as background for a more particularized identity. Rather, an effect of individuality emerges from negotiations—by readers as well as characters—with representations of groups and types. In particular, the Victorian novel, like the synthetic constructions of nineteenth-century statisticians, mediates the individual identities and emotions of readers through representations of the lives of imaginary others.[8] Adapting a phrase from Franco Moretti, whose attempt to reorient literary criticism in quantitative terms I discuss in detail below, I refer to the experiencing and tracking of individual emotion constructed and enabled by such representations as "distant reading," in which what appears as distance is the organization of identity into culturally coherent categories and emotional systems, enabling a reading of the self—including that which seems most deeply personal about the self, such as the nature of one's happiness—as if viewed from without. Of distance's clarifying power, Moretti writes, "distance is [however] not an obstacle . . . but a *specific form of knowledge:* fewer elements, hence a sharper sense of their overall connection" (1; emphasis in original). This "sharper sense," I argue, is sharpened by exclusion: the reduction of the many to the few creates narrative; the elimination of idiosyncracies produces a simplified and readable trajectory.

In *The Politics of Large Numbers,* Alain Desrosières describes the way statistics create new political spaces and the appearance of a new reality.

> Creating a political space involves and makes possible the erection of a space of common measurement, within which things may be compared, because the categories and encoding procedures are identical. . . . Reality appears as the product of a series of material recordings: the more general the recordings—in other words, the more firmly established the conventions of equivalence on which they are founded, as a result of broader investments—the greater the reality of the product. . . . The aim of statistics is to reduce the abundance of situations and to provide a summarized description of them that can be remembered and used as a basis for action. (9–13)

The aim of statistics, Desrosières argues, is to produce consensus: "forms that everyone can agree on" (16).[9] The Victorian novel is arguably the nineteenth century's most supple vehicle for the circulation of such forms: not, of course, in the sense that readers or critics necessarily agree about a text's interpretation, but rather in the form's own reliance on the consent of numerous readers to particular conventions for representing character and identity. Thus while it may seem correct to claim, as Poovey does, that "the conventions of literature elevated individualizing narratives over the kind of aggregation used in government blue books" (*Social Body,* 17), this can be the case only when the nature of the aggregate has been so completely assimilated as to be taken for granted. Indeed, despite the genre's much-celebrated focus on individuality and idiosyncracy, the Victorian novel often construes individual character and emotion as a degree of similarity to or difference from a norm, just as statisticians create the possibility of viewing reality as a system of perturbations from an average.[10] To say this is not to propose that characters in Victorian fiction lack the distinctiveness or eccentricity long admired by readers and critics, but rather to refocus the argument, familiar from the work of Michel Foucault, that sees the emergence of categories of deviance in the nineteenth century as the effect of a new insistence on the normal.[11] For the narrowing of possibilities entailed by the prominence of certain cultural narratives, such as that of financial success versus ruin, or the achievement of happiness versus a fall into unhappiness—like the structure of deviance from the norm in Foucault's work—supplies the Victorian novel with its dominant interests and chief ideological work: the careful teasing out of fine psychological and emotional distinctions that draw their meaning from a series of narratives and characterological structures whose premises remain unarticulated and therefore, often, unchallenged. Such generalizations about character function as interpellating structures, reinforcing specific cultural narratives as constitutive of identity per se. And they also give rise to new narratives: when the average man or woman begins to circulate in the cultural imagination, for instance, characters in novels—such as George Eliot's *Middlemarch*—begin to perceive themselves in relation to the average. Or, in Trollope's *The Prime Minister* (as in other novels of the period, such as *The Way We Live Now, Little Dorrit,* and *Our Mutual Friend*) a wide range of social concerns, resulting in what Galton might call "disarray," are assimilated to and ostensibly resolved by a narrative that finds coherence in the difference between the character of the speculator and that of the investor. Associations between character and the stock market; the habits and requirements of an "average" life; the idea of happiness as a measurable substance (an idea that continues to be promoted by the quantitative ethos of twentieth- and twenty-first-century "happiness economics")—these and other concepts, naturalized and vivified through cultural repetition and novelistic representation, shake off their constructed status: their origins in the imposition of a conceptual grid.

The literal presence of the graph is not required by the readings presented here. Though graphs were used in statistics and finance in nineteenth-century England, they were not the ubiquitous presence in the popular press they have since become, and I make no claim to find actual graphs in *Middlemarch* or *David Copperfield.* As I discuss in my second chapter, the changing status of share prices has long been a topic of intense public interest; as Desrosières points out, the social policies created with the use of graphs, not the graphs themselves, influence political decisions and contribute to the formation of social realities. Nevertheless, I contend that the figure of the graph—and not only the stock-market graph—projects the skeletal form or deep structure of a pervasive quantifying and consolidating vision that not only represents the individual's assimilation to the mass or group but also assists in that assimilation, in a manner similar to that which Terry Castle has ascribed to eighteenth-century barometers and thermometers as instruments that both reflect new ways of conceptualizing emotion and, in material form, contribute to its reconceptualization.[12] The graph thus functions in this book not, primarily, as the culmination of a historical trajectory, but rather as an exceptionally clear picture of a persistent, fantasmatic system—as compellingly coherent for us as it was for the Victorians—in which dissimilar elements are assimilated to a new reality; value and identity are created; and individual elements are linked in an apparently coherent system by virtue of their comparison to one another.

The Average[13]

Nineteenth-century strategies of quantification and measurement often arranged diverse natural and social phenomena, including details of physical appearance and the information about character those details ostensibly revealed, on theoretical scales, with individual elements positioned for the purpose of comparison around an imaginary mid-point: a composite or average devised to anchor the system. One well-known example is Alphonse Bertillon's systematization of criminal types, originally based on comparisons between photographs of criminal suspects and photographs from Bertillon's archive of criminal portraits. As Armstrong points out, when an increasing number of cases rendered the matching process unmanageable, Bertillon began to measure bodily parts and facial features "in terms of their distance from an abstract average," creating "the categories for a filing system that could quickly be consulted for a match. . . . The police no longer matched photograph to photograph; instead, they matched photographs to an idealized image which began to seem more primary than either individuals or their portraits" (17–18).[14] That is, turning persons into statistical representations—measuring the proportions of body parts he deemed representative—Bertillon transformed those representations into a coherent whole, indeed a character: a personification in relation to which identity—in this case, criminal identity—was imagined and constructed.[15] This particular idea of the average, for Bertillon, thus underwrote the social reality and ideological construction known as criminality. But Armstrong's more general discussion of Victorian realism and photography, drawing on Foucauldian and Lacanian accounts of the way subject formation "begins with an identification with an image and involves [them in] a lifelong attempt to maintain that relationship" (24), also suggests that rather than being unique, these genres are particularly powerful examples of a much larger and more diffuse system of relational accounts of identity: a system that is not too far from imagining every individual as a composite, each physical or characterological feature supposed to exemplify the qualities of a specific population.[16] Members of a culture intent on quantifying and classifying its population and what it defines as its significant attributes could thus generally be said to possess mental versions of Bertillon's filing systems, in relation to which they more or less reflexively construct their own identities. Assigning to abstractions numbers, relative positions, or, as Bertillon did, pictures, vivifies them, endowing terms such as "criminality" or "intelligence" (or, as I discuss later, happiness) with social reality and ideological power.

In 1840s France, averages were commonly used in commerce, mathematics, and physics. Adolphe Quetelet applied the laws of physics and astronomy to human society; in particular, he sought to apply statistical principles of stability over time to seemingly irrational and disorderly social events such as drunkenness and crime. Like Galton, Quetelet mapped his vision metaphorically, and his language evokes an image of moving bodies: he imagined that individuals "oscillate" between extremes, and envisioned a figure who would represent a "state of equilibrium . . . distant from excesses and defects of every kind" (Porter, *Rise* 103). Quetelet's vision, again like Galton's, maps the individual human form onto an abstract image of an idealized whole; it also offers an image of economic and emotional balance, the one conceived in direct relation to the other.[17] As Theodore Porter writes, "Quetelet held that great inequalities of wealth and vast price fluctuations were responsible for crime and turmoil; he exalted the life of moderation, unaffected by sudden passions, and conjectured that the 'higher classes' live longer than the 'low people' not because of wealth or nutrition, but because of their 'habits of propriety, of temperance, of passions excited less frequently and variations less sudden in their manner of existence'" (*Rise* 103). Quetelet's average man was a statistical solution to a social problem, a "mean" who was ideal not because he exceeded the qualities of the average, but rather because he embodied them. Neither too much nor too little, he was, in effect, a codification of the imaginary being who functions to this day as the implicit subject of bourgeois societies, the least common denominator in relation to whom these societies are constructed.[18]

An ideal of balance similar to Quetelet's—linking the economic and the emotional—appears in the 1870s in the work of William Stanley Jevons, one of several figures who sought to transform economics into a mathematical science in nineteenth-century England. Jevons, trained as a gold assayer, derived his economic theory from the Benthamite idea that people fundamentally seek pleasure and avoid pain; his goal was to apply mechanical ideas of balance to human emotion, thereby arriving at a scientific theory of supply and demand. Feeling itself, Jevons wrote, could not be measured, but consumption could, and for him the dynamic of production and consumption offered a tangible, material manifestation of otherwise ineffable impulses. Moreover, as if in possession of internal weighing scales or teeter-totters, people were for Jevons in a state of constantly and automatically assessing and adjusting their own equilibrium.

> A unit of pleasure or pain is difficult even to conceive; but it is the amount of these feelings which is continually prompting us to buying and selling, borrowing and lending, labouring and resting, producing and consuming; and it is from the quantitative effects of the feelings that we must estimate their comparative amounts. We can no more know nor measure gravity in its own nature than we can measure a feeling; but, just as we measure gravity by its effects in the motion of a pendulum, so we may estimate the equality or inequality of feelings by the decisions of the human mind. The will is our pendulum, and its oscillations are minutely registered in the price lists of the markets. (17)

These oscillations and the balance they seem to seek are for Jevons not mathematically determined but rather intuited; they represent the internalization—the equivalent in feeling—of an economic principle. As one of Jevons's critics puts it, "Just as someone could roughly perceive the equilibrium of a balance with the eye, so the individual was able to judge the equivalence of pleasures and pains by paying attention only to their marginal increase or decrease. No assumption was needed as to whether the mind was able to judge accurately numerical quantities of utility. It was only necessary to assume that the mind could perceive a rough equivalence (or inequality) between them . . . Jevons's utility theory rested on measurement without numbers" (Maas 296).

Jevons and Quetelet envision a relationship between the individual and the group such that a theory for one is a theory for all; they seek a figure or set of numbers that will prove regular and predictable. And both are aware, at the same time, that individuals tend to deviate from the models and ideals established in their name. Indeed, wrote Quetelet,

> It is of primary importance to keep out of view man as he exists in an insulated, separate, individual state, and to regard him only as a fraction of the species . . . we may instance the case of a person examining too nearly a small portion of a very large circle, and who, consequently, would see in this detached portion merely a certain quantity of physical points. . . . But, placing himself at a greater distance, the eye embraces of necessity a greater number of points, and already a greater degree of regularity is observable over a certain extent of the segment of the circle; and, by removing still farther from the object, the observer loses sight of the individual points, no longer observes any accidental or odd arrangements amongst them, but discovers at once the law presiding over their general arrangements, and the precise nature of the circle so traced. But let us suppose, as might happen, that the different points of the arch, instead of being material points, were small animated beings, free to act according to their will . . . these spontaneous motions would not be perceived by the eye placed at a suitable distance. (5)

Providing a way out of the difficulty caused by the failure of any single entity to adhere to general laws—the problem of perceiving, rather than a clear pattern, "merely a certain quantity of physical points"—was a rule derived within astronomy and later applied to biology and the social sciences, by means of which "great numbers of observations" could be reduced to "a single value or curve" (Porter, *Rise* 95). Using this strategy of distant reading, known as the error law, statisticians and scientists constructed universal rules from a plethora of observational data, revealing what they construed as the true pattern or curve the data would assume were all errors of observation and calculation (in other words, all actual observers) eliminated. (Thus in order for Galton to calculate his flowing curve he had no need to line up the members of any given population in order of height, but could instead deduce their theoretical measurements from two numbers: the lowest and the highest.) The resulting curve need not be, and is not, a representation of actual individuals; rather, it is the projection of a "law" of statistics that, keeping individual differences "out of view," yields the discovery of a regular pattern. Despite their different forms, Quetelet's circle resembles Galton's graph, both in its mapping of persons onto points and in its search for regular form: the effacing of "accidental" or "odd" arrangements—social disarray—to yield an aesthetically pleasing image of the social whole.

In Quetelet's description of the circle and the points out of which it is made, individuals are not only envisioned as harmonious parts of a larger system, but they are also—as members of such a system—imagined as including within themselves some aspect of the whole: the animated beings visible at a distance, that is, must have internalized the circle's orderly principle. Thus it makes sense that Quetelet proposed the existence of a relationship between society and the individual such that, were criminal acts recorded throughout society, "the average man could be assigned a 'penchant for crime' equal to the number of criminal acts committed divided by the population" (Porter, *Rise* 53). The penchant, that is, comes not from the individual but is rather derived from society, which "includes within itself the germs of all the crimes committed, and at the same time the necessary facilities for their development. . . . It is the social state . . . which prepares these crimes, and the criminal is merely the instrument to execute them" (Quetelet 6). Thus "the propensity of the average man to commit a crime or become drunk could be calculated as the arrest or drunkenness rate for the group in question . . . " (Stigler 170). Society, or the social, inhabits the individual, rather than the other way around. Similarly, Jevons's work includes the unifying image of a "trading body": "any number of people whose aggregate influence in a market, either in the way of supply or demand, we have to consider. . . . The trading body may be a single individual in one case; it may be the whole inhabitants of a continent in another; it may be the individuals of a trade diffused through a country in a third. . . . the principles of exchange are the same in nature, however wide or narrow may be the market considered. Every trading body is either an individual or an aggregate of individuals, and the law, in the case of the aggregate, must depend upon the fulfilment of law in the individuals" (88–89). As in the case of Bertillon's composites, the individual and the group are figured as reflexive, each a version of the other. Giving the group priority over the individual, these theorists maintain the concept of the individual, but in a new form: each person is now fungible, possessing characteristics interchangeable with those of the larger society. In these configurations, society does not take its character from the unique qualities of its members, but has rather become a template for the construction of individuals, who draw their separate characters from it. In this formulation, which takes shape in a variety of ways in the texts I discuss here, a character is imagined as having internalized a composite image of the social whole in the form of the average man; the stock market; or a unifying, synthetic representation of happiness.

The Market

The systems described above—those of Bertillon, Galton, Quetelet, and Jevons—differ in emphasis and detail: Bertillon was interested in criminality; Galton in heredity and genius; Quetelet in the average man, and Jevons in the movement of prices. But they share the strategy that, borrowing from Moretti, I want to call distant reading: the organization and consolidation of information so that individual differences yield to an image of the harmonious working-together of diverse elements. For Quetelet, people are regulated by invisible forces and automatically seek a balance between extremes; for Jevons, character, goods, and prices objectify human emotions, representing an achievement of or failure to achieve balance. These objectifications seem to express the ineffable or unrepresentable (we cannot "measure a feeling," Jevons writes). But representations (as in, "the price lists of the markets") are not, in my argument, secondary—the expression of preexisting feeling—but rather primary, shaping the narratives of emotion they are said to reflect: indeed, shaping the cultural product known as emotion.

For Galton, the figure of the bell curve suggests the translation into reality of the phenomenon it has been created to describe: the possibility of an orderly and organized population. For the figure pictured at the beginning of my third chapter—the man with a stock-ticker for a heart—the imagined internalization of the market suggests an intuitive apprehension of changes in the prices of stocks and shares: an immediate, visceral knowledge of what others "like" him are doing with their money. But those numbers, like the figure of the graph that comes to represent them, are not (once again) representations of individuals, but synthetic qualities. Summarizing multifarious, distinct activities, they create a new reality—the reality of the market—as a series of deviations from a norm. And the identities and actions that seem to be embodied by the stock exchange or stock market, from the nineteenth century to the twenty-first, are similarly the projected effects of the activities of numerous individuals refashioned in the image of a composite body or character.

The stock-market graph is not the only representation of such a system, but it is probably the one most immediately recognizable to a modern audience, symbolically linking the individual experiences of those who attend to it (as well as those who do not) with an external image purporting to represent the collective effect of their actions; aligning the rhythm of separate hearts and pulses with a coherent emotional narrative. Again, the figure of the graph merely externalizes a rhetorical function the exchange or market is already assumed to display: changes in the prices of stocks and shares were tracked with increasing fervor from the 1840s on, as economic journalism created an imagined community of readers who saw in these figures a reflection of their collective material and emotional condition.[19] Thus the market and the graph that comes to represent it take shape as striking instances—indeed, overdeterminations—of the kind of vivified abstraction described above, representing a variety of identities and activities as similar and hence comparable; tying emotional and bodily responses to the rise and fall of prices in a self-reinforcing circulation of elements that contributes to their apparent inevitability (the market as mirror). Indeed, if Bertillon's criminal type functioned as a social reality for the Victorians, and Galton's mathematics similarly rendered comprehensible what would otherwise appear chaotic and unassimilable, the stock market may be said to function for the Victorians and for us in much the same way: as a simple trajectory, indeed a character, endowing what would otherwise be a disparate collection of activities and events with coherence and intention.

In market societies, stock prices are often represented as the objective form of the emotions of persons commonly referred to as investors; stockmarket discourse thus constructs both character and emotion in stockmarket terms. Popular renderings of economic events link emotional and physical responses to the already personified figure of a national economy; feelings are said to grow or diminish with the tempo and intensity of prices, and people are said to possess qualities defining them as either investors or speculators—not just in their dealings with stocks and shares, but in other areas of life as well.[20] Imagined as oscillating between these two characterological poles, stock-market representations externalize character traits, or impulses, those who attend to the market are imagined as having internalized; like the idea of a criminal type, the stock market owes its social reality, power, and agency to collective belief in that internalization. Consolidating the actions and intentions of innumerable individual elements, the market is a mass character, the imagined embodiment of an average man.[21]

Happiness

Darrin McMahon's *A History of Happiness*—one of a spate of happiness books published in the early 2000s—begins by asserting that, "Given . . . the immense difficulty, even impossibility, of ever judging another's state of happiness with precision (indeed, of judging one's own), I have chosen instead to focus on representations of the term and concept as these have developed over time" (10). But this recourse to representation merely reinforces what "everyone" knows to be the case: that even as its contents are said to be endlessly variable—capable of being defined differently by each individual—happiness has long functioned as a single term or universal value. Indeed, the pressure often exerted on the term happiness, in Victorian cultural discourse as in our own—the amount of ideological work it is called upon to do—suggests that it functions (as height does for Galton or share prices for the stock market) as a conceptual tool, organizing identity within the terms of a specific cultural narrative.

I am not concerned here with happiness as a quality—what happiness "is" or might be—but rather with happiness as an idea that, like the other terms and constructions discussed throughout this book, produces an effect of both individual and social coherence. As in the examples of the average man and the stock market, I am interested in the way happiness functions as a summary or averaging term, tying together disparate events and experiences in a manner that creates the unity it purports to describe. Just as, in Jeremy Bentham's felicific calculus, the imagining of happiness as measurable dissolves individual identities into an ideally coherent image of the social whole, so too does the word "happiness" dissolve particular experiences into coherent form. Happiness is not unique in this: other emotional categories function similarly. But the term is particularly relevant to this book's concerns because, for example, of its ideological function as an idealized average around which novelistic characters are arranged and a prize for which they vie; because of stock-market rhetoric's alignment of prices with emotional ups and downs; and because of the logic of equivalence and substitution that governs the relationship between happiness and money in Victorian novels and cultural discourse.

Feelings, Emotions, Affect

Taking on the term "affect," Eve Sedgwick has criticized work in the field of affect studies for naming as its object an undifferentiated whole—treating affect "as a unitary category, with a unitary history and a unitary politics" (110, 112). More specifically, Visvathan Soni argues that in the eighteenth century happiness becomes "'reified' in the strict sense of the word: that it becomes a thing, rather than a judgment about the complexity and heterogeneity of a narrative. This 'thing' acquires the fundamental determination of an affect, *abstracted* from narrative" (emphasis in original).[22] Both critiques suggest the way generally unacknowledged transformations in discourse construct new objects of analysis and identifications, constituting unity as an effect of representation. "'Discrepancies and interruptions,' in an undifferentiated flow of 'arousal,'" writes Sedgwick, quoting one such example from the 1987 *Oxford Companion to the Mind*, "have a reassuringly mechanical, Morse code-like sound: no danger whatever, here, of encountering the fallacy that a representation might bear any nonarbitrary relation to the thing represented" (112).

Attuned to this problematic, Sarah Ahmed focuses on the "objects" of emotion rather than emotion itself, arguing that feelings only seem to reside in objects, to be something we "have." Her discussion of the sociality of emotions, and especially of the way feeling may be said to come "from without" rather than within—as "what hold or binds the social body together"—meshes with my sense of the way the term "happiness" is used, in the texts and cultural discourses I discuss here, to unify and solidify diverse experiences (9–11). As an account of "how we become invested in social norms" and a critique of the privatization and psychologization of emotion, Ahmed's work, like Soni's, suggests that the objectification of feeling naturalizes social and political effects.[23] This section of the book thus highlights my focus not on the material reality of the graph, but rather on the effects of the conceptual grid that invisibly underlies it: the identification of a mid-point or average around which separate elements are grouped; the appeal to a single, cohesive term as a means of assimilating diverse elements to a single scale. These concepts, I suggest, are present in the use of the term "happiness" in John Stuart Mill's *Autobiography* and Dickens's *David Copperfield*.

The association of happiness with representation in Mill and Dickens—specifically with idealized representations of Victorian domesticity—defines an identification with a fantasmatic unity, a positioning of the social (a familiar image of ideological consensus) "within" the individual. Implicitly appealing to an internalized—and what, in my discussion of *Middlemarch*, I refer to as an idealized—average, the word refers to an affective experience that, defined in individual terms, also signals the individual's absorption of and alignment with the group. The contemporary field of happiness economics, intent on quantifying individual and collective happiness, takes the Victorian tendency to quantify emotion to its logical endpoint, affirming, by surrounding with an aura of scientific authority, the reality of a cultural narrative in which members of a disparate population possessing diverse ideas of happiness may see themselves collectively reflected. Thus objectified, happiness is aligned with, and implicitly designates, various objects of desire, such as money or a particular kind of family, and becomes—or rather is revealed to be, for I argue that *David Copperfield* anticipates the findings of sociologists and happiness researchers in this area—an object of competition: something, as Bentham discovered, whose susceptibility to averaging simply conceals its unequal distribution.[24] Ideologically constructed in opposition to the fixedness of birth and inherited status as supremely flexible—adaptable to individual needs—Victorian happiness nevertheless displays a fixedness of its own.

———

THE CHAPTERS that follow explore the representation and construction of emotion and identity in selected Victorian novels and cultural discourses in relation to collective, vivified abstractions: unified representations of the many. They highlight connections between twentieth- and twenty-first century representations and Victorian ones, emphasizing continuities rather than differences in order to demonstrate the Victorian lineage of—and thereby denaturalize—both Victorian and contemporary truisms about, for instance, the relation between character and the stock market, or the quantitative nature of emotion. Widely-accepted contemporary accounts of emotion and identity are, I suggest, indebted to Victorian structures of quantification, and I situate readings of Victorian texts in relation to contemporary examples—stock-market advice, the idea of "happiness economics"—in order to render the nature and extent of that debt explicit.[25]

The examples offered here are not intended to be comprehensive, nor could they be; they are meant instead to highlight a persistent tendency— one, I argue, we share with the Victorians—to define the self as an effect (indeed, a personification) of quantitative representations. This emphasis on quantification ties emotion to money, as a substance whose fungibility renders it endlessly available as a signifier of character and at the same time reinforces the idea of character itself as measurable. But money is only one kind of quantification, and characters in Victorian novels tend to be arranged on different kinds of comparative scales. My opening chapter, for instance, finds in *Middlemarch* a hierarchy of characters founded on their capacity for emotional intensity; the novel's more interesting characters are "set off" against the more commonplace or ordinary. The consciousnesses of the more interesting are thus formed in relation to the less interesting; indeed, as in the case of Quetelet's penchant or that of Bertillon's criminals, characters are represented as having formed their identities in relation to ideologically charged images of the mass or the group. The identities of these characters thus emerge as effects of their engagement with representations of collective or average identities.

In the two chapters at the book's center, the idea of the average, discussed in chapter 1, and of that of happiness, discussed in chapter 4, intertwine in the rhetoric of the stock market and the stock-market graph. The market, I argue, is rhetorically constructed as an average man, a collective reflection of feeling and identity that structures emotion as synthetic, one-dimensional, and trackable. While I do not wish to argue that capitalist ideology negates the possibility of any ideology outside the economic, and indeed locate in this book a more basic conceptual grid in the general idea of quantification, the stock market emerges here as an overdetermined effect: a structure in which representations of emotion, identity, and money circulate and reinforce one another to create a powerful social reality.

These chapters discuss the development of a discourse of impulse and restraint that finds coherence in the assigning of different approaches to the market to different emotional states and types of characters. Just as Galton's curve transforms the incomprehensible and chaotic into the beautiful, so too does the articulation of clearly defined, strictly opposed emotions and the character types said to embody them domesticate and transform into narrative what might otherwise appear as a series of discontinuous and diversely motivated transactions. The process of identification and differentiation described above takes shape primarily as an opposition between investment and speculation, as the stock exchange and the graph that comes to represent it shape the idea of tracking, or distantly reading, individual and collective emotions. Thus chapter 2 traces a historical archive wherein changes in the prices of stock and shares came to be inscribed in the bodies of individual investors, as hearts and pulses are said to echo what is defined, reciprocally—in the mirroring structure Rancière and Althusser characterize as ideologically constitutive—as the somatic rhythm of the market's fluctuations.

Stock-market discourse constructs and maintains the market's authority in part by referring moral distinctions to stock-market roles. But the characteristics this rhetoric defines as psychologically distinct in fact describe a continuum, suggesting the source of the market's apparently unending need for external regulation: the insistence that the scrupulous be separated from the unscrupulous in a repeated insistence on objective distinctions in character and action. The opposition between the investor, who projects his identity calmly and prudently into the future, and the speculator, who requires immediate gratification and transgresses against both moral and legal boundaries in the attempt to fulfill his desires, both assists in the translation of market activity into characterological form and also organizes and legitimates that activity. This difference is often, in the novels I discuss here, resolved in favor of a middle position that offsets them both, in which the temporal structure of a character's needs and desires overlaps with the familiar tenets of Victorian domestic ideology, and is finally resolved in favor of an idealized image of the familial and domestic: the life of the average (family) man. This chapter also describes the way differences in character are founded in a circular system of reference, as in the way in which one member of the stock exchange vouches for the character of another, or the manner in which the market relies on and reinforces novelistic structures of character while the novel draws on the ostensible reality of market categories. A discussion of the way the capacity for restraint defines not just stock-market activity but character in general in Dickens's *Little Dorrit* paves the way for a more detailed reading of the use of investment and speculation as an organizing trope in Trollope's *The Prime Minister*.

Chapter 3 raises the topic of happiness in its account of Ferdinand Lopez's "irrational exuberance": his attachment of his own emotions, and the novel's attachment of his value, to the financial market's characterological system. Tracking the prices of shares, Lopez aligns himself with a narrative of averages: representations of coherence generated from numerous and diverse financial transactions. That these transactions are understood as representations or reflections of emotion exemplifies in vivid terms what Desrosières has called the reality generated by the idea of the average: the naturalizing of economic forces through the association of individual and collective feeling with specific linear structures; the insinuation or interpellation of generalized effects in individual bodies and emotions. Assimilating its romantic narrative to stock-market feelings, *The Prime Minister* not only punishes Lopez for speculating with money, but it also provides Emily Wharton with a template for her romantic narrative, in which investment in emotion is regarded as preferable to speculation in it. The rise and fall of Lopez's shares, like that of Micawber's income and of David Copperfield's happiness, offers a tangible image of and explanation for the flutterings and fluctuations that, traced to individual bodies, appear as their natural and inevitable reflection.

Because my reading of *David Copperfield* draws together issues discussed elsewhere in the book—the average man of *Middlemarch;* Lopez's irrational exuberance; the romantic speculations of another Emily—I depart here from the novels' own chronology, placing it after discussions of *Middlemarch, Little Dorrit,* and *The Prime Minister.* This chapter ties the use of the term "happiness" in Dickens's novel to John Stuart Mill's autobiographical account of his emotional crisis: a crisis prompted by the question about his own happiness he notoriously posed to himself. Mill's famous assertion that success in reforming the world would not, as he had imagined, make him happy, like David Copperfield's insistent references to what I have dubbed "happiness moments," is tied to happiness's status as an abstraction Victorian domestic ideology offers to fulfill in concrete form. For Mill and David Copperfield, I argue, happiness names an identification with culturally-defined representations, one rendered explicit by a textual structure in which the term summons up a scene or series of scenes within which a subject sees himself. Referring happiness to representations, these texts construct happiness and the self that experiences it vicariously; associating the term with specific images, including rooms and families, they locate at the center of an ostensibly individualized expression of feeling a shared image of middle-class domesticity. The term "happiness" as used in these texts thus draws on what I referred to earlier as a conceptual grid, organizing experience into a simple and ideologically useful narrative. And this grid also, as the chapter discusses in greater detail, constructs happiness as money's symbolic equivalent. Like *Middlemarch, David Copperfield* highlights Victorian culture's anxious focus on happiness as a gauge of middle-class status: in Lydgate's inability to separate himself from the commonness he defines as an obstacle to his success; in the attention Mill and David Copperfield bestow on their individual emotional economies; in a general attempt—characteristic of the Victorian novel—to replace money with happiness as middle-class identity's chief currency.

My conclusion could have taken several different forms. It is not difficult, for instance, to point toward the persistence in contemporary discourse of simplified narratives tying individual emotion to a narrative of collective identity, as in the identification of fluctuations in mood with those of stocks and shares. In Jonathan Frantzen's *The Corrections,* for instance, "The more Alfred saw of the Erie Belt, the more distinctly he felt the Midland Pacific's superior size, strength, and moral vitality in his own limbs and carriage." Frantzen's investment banker, Gary, attends to the rise and fall of his "mental markets—glycemic, endocrine, over-the-synapse," while his brother Chip has the sense that, "In a matter of seconds, like a market inundated by a wave of panic selling, he was plunged into shame and self-consciousness" (243; 189; 157). Or: the evocative image of the graph appears frequently in advertisements, as in one representation that maps the wavering line of an EKG onto an identical figure said to represent an automobile engine's RPM, accompanied by text encouraging readers to "be the car." Both these examples suggest the assimilation of individual responses—somatic, emotional—to collective narratives: that of the stock market, on the one hand, that of consumer culture on the other—the latter aligning the driver's heart with the automobile's engine in a perfect synchronicity of man and machine. My decision to focus on Moretti's work stems in part from his application of the graph to literary criticism, in part from the way his use of the graph as a unifying abstraction, offered as a new critical model, both echoes nineteenth-century accounts of the aesthetic pleasure offered by statistical constructions and, in an alignment of personal, collective, and literary history, attests to the continued seductiveness of this figure's invitation to locate the self within its trajectory.

The average man of my title is thus not the figure novel theory refers to as a "type," nor does he represent a general notion of a typical person or a mathematically precise idea of an average. Rather, his is an affective life that participates in, because it is made up of, other individuals "like" himself: representations of a social whole in which, in what is finally a *mise-en-abyme* of identity-making, he sees himself reflected.

CHAPTER ONE

Middlemarch
The Affective Life of the Average Man

Old provincial society had its share of this subtle movement: had not only its
striking downfalls, its brilliant young professional dandies who ended by living
up an entry with a drab and six children for their establishment, but also those
less marked vicissitudes which are constantly shifting the boundaries of social
intercourse, and begetting new consciousness of interdependence. Some slipped
a little downward, some got higher footing . . . a few personages or families that
stood with rock firmness amid all this fluctuation, were slowly presenting new
aspects in spite of solidity, and altering with the double change of self and beholder.
(George Eliot, *Middlemarch*)

The following scene appears early in George Eliot's *Middlemarch:*

> The casket was soon open before them, and the various jewels spread
> out, making a bright parterre on the table. It was no great collection,
> but a few of the ornaments were really of remarkable beauty, the finest
> that was obvious at first being a necklace of purple amethysts set in
> exquisite gold-work, and a pearl cross with five brilliants in it. Dorothea
> immediately took up the necklace and fastened it round her sister's
> neck, where it fitted almost as closely as a bracelet; but the circle suited
> the Henrietta-Maria style of Celia's head and neck, and she could see
> that it did, in the pier-glass opposite. (34)

The jewels are, of course, an allegory, considered in their settings as the
women are considered in theirs. Dorothea and Celia assess them in that
function, as frameworks for the wearer's complexion and clothing, show-
ing both to advantage as they themselves (the jewels) are set off in their
metal fixtures: "There, Celia, you can wear that with your Indian muslin.
But this cross you must wear with your dark dresses." At the same time

we learn that "souls have complexions too" (35), as Dorothea rejects altogether her own wearing of the jewels—and hence their effect in the scene is also to assist in the setting off of one sister from another.

The idea of "setting off" informs Eliot's novel at several levels: from its first sentence, which tells us that "Miss Brooke had that kind of beauty which seems to be thrown into relief by poor dress" (29), to its character system, in which some characters set off others—as Celia in this scene, with her ordinary vanity, provides a backdrop for her sister's more exalted variety. Indeed, in *Middlemarch* it is the function of the many to set off the few, since only in this way can the qualities of the latter be perceived: if "Mrs. Casaubon is too unlike other women for them to be compared with her" (474), for example, the novel never troubles to explore the particular qualities of those other women with whom Mrs. Casaubon might mistakenly be compared. Particular qualities are, in fact, precisely what Eliot's language suggests these women lack. The rhetorical constructions that condense the many into a homogenous mass—the word "other," in "other women"; "every," as in, "You have not the same tastes as every young lady" (64), or the impersonal articles identifying Sir James Chettam as "just *the* sort of man *a* woman would like" (63; my emphasis) consign much of humanity to the category of likeness within which Chettam—or, as the novel often refers to him, "a fellow like Chettam" (63)—resides.[1]

Eliot's novel has long been the subject of the kind of sociological interest its subtitle, "a study of provincial life," invites. But with a central character diagnosed as suffering from "a love of extremes" (31), and a plot that revolves around the inexorable influence of the mediocre middle on those who would distinguish themselves from it, the novel also illustrates in exemplary fashion the conceptual and affective consequences of what had, by the time of its writing, attained the status of an intuitive truth: that in order for some individuals to be exceptional, others must embody the roles of median, midpoint, lowest common denominator. *Middlemarch* fleshes out the never very abstract abstractions of the nineteenth-century statistical imagination: an imagination in which the idea of the average begins to appear in the form of a person.

The Problem of Likeness

Tracing the concept of the average in political science and economic thought, Alain Desrosières points toward the existence of "intuitive" examples in eighteenth-century discourse: phrases demonstrating a cognitive "leap from one level to another," in which commonality and likeness replace physical and temporal disparity and difference. Such phrases as "when all is said and done" and "the strong carrying the weak," writes Desrosières, appear in generalizations about agricultural production across diverse geographical areas and time spans, replacing "local singularities" with "a new object of a general order," evincing a desire to find a quantity "between two extremes" (72). In such examples, he argues, the average appears not as a mathematical or scientific notion but rather as an affective and ideological one, the solution to an emotional and cognitive dilemma. These homilies articulate a desire for emotional stability, equity, and balance; for a whole rather than a series of parts; for a stable vantage point. They—and the idea of the average per se—might be said to offer the solace of a perspective described by the eighteenth-century mathematician Jacob Bernouilli as somewhere between "the best we can hope for and the worst we can expect" (Klein 144). Indeed, in the nineteenth century—a period whose enthusiasm for quantification of many kinds is well known—the use of averages could be considered a response to the effect Kant dubbed the mathematical sublime: the condition of being overwhelmed by the perception of an unassimilably large collection of things. And one such collection, in an era of heightened social competition and mobility, might well consist of the numerous members of a class or group whose representation, in an era that emphasized the construction of identity as a function of social coordinates—details of class status, income, and occupation—rendered them disturbingly similar to oneself.[2]

It is a commonplace of *Middlemarch* criticism that the central characters of Eliot's novel are under pressure to differentiate themselves from the town's "petty medium," which surrounds and threatens to engulf them, eliminating any traces of distinctiveness. Extraordinary individuals such as Dorothea and Lydgate are powerless against this medium, which is often identified as history itself, specifically the nineteenth century. The nineteenth century is said to be at fault in the form, for instance, of the limited context for female ambition that makes a St. Theresa-like kind of greatness impossible for her would-be later representative. But other issues are relevant as well, not least the manner in which, as the novel points out most specifically with reference to Lydgate, the failure to resist mediocrity is said to have an internal cause in a character's identification with the common. "The ego awakens to three facts at once," writes Calvin Bedient, describing the absorption of Eliot's characters by and of the community: "its own insignificance, its desecration of the community, and its inadmissibility as a principle of being. It then empties itself out, filling the vacuum with the collective" (Bedient 46). But in Eliot's conception of character in *Middlemarch*, identity is already emptied out and filled with the collective: shaped by a formulation that, in the manner of the statistically-formed average man who becomes a part of common consciousness in the nineteenth century, situates the many within the one and makes of that one an element (or "unit," to use one of the novel's terms) in a larger pool. Character in *Middlemarch* is in its essence comparative; more than that, it emerges distinctly as a felt relation to the collective. In Eliot's novel, as in statistical formulations, "character" is made up of—or found to be lacking in—elements that emerge as significant because they have been identified as the characteristics of a group. Not least in the experience it offers its readers, but in its mapping of character relations and rhetoric of character description as well, Eliot's novel represents, reproduces, and recreates a sense of what it feels like to be a statistic: the affective life of the average man.[3]

Nineteenth-century statistics confronted, as statistics continues to do, a contradiction: individuals could be analyzed individually, on an empirical and experiential level, or they could be assessed as a group on the basis of selected qualities they were held to possess in common. Debates arose around the difficulty of reconciling the contingent, random nature of individual examples with the regular distribution (such as the consistent rates of births, marriages, and deaths in a given population) perceived in the group. In 1835 in France, Adolphe Quetelet provided a means of reconciling such apparently irreconcilable differences: they could be explained, as Desrosières writes, "if one assumed the existence, beyond these individual contingent cases, of an *average man,* of which these cases were imperfect copies" (75–76). Measuring the distance of individual examples from a mathematically-derived norm using what is now called a bell curve, Quetelet posited a fictional being who served as a perfect model or midpoint in relation to which all other beings could be imagined. Particular individuals were distributed "around" this average man in the same manner that, Quetelet reasoned in an illustrative example, a Prussian king, "filled with admiration for a statue of a gladiator, ordered a thousand copies to be made by a thousand sculptors in his kingdom. Their sculptures were not perfect, and their works were distributed with deviations from the model, in much the same way that particular individuals were distributed around the average man. The Creator was then equivalent to the King of Prussia, and individuals were imperfect realizations of a perfect model" (Desrosières 75–76). In a formulation that would seem to differ significantly from Eliot's, and from our contemporary one as well, Quetelet imagined the average as an ideal: an admirably moderate, "balanced" individual.[4] But whether considered ideal or not, the positing of such "middle" figures as reference points figures largely in the construction of nineteenth-century character, in the novel as well as in statistics.

The average man thus emerged in statistical science as an attempt to unify the disparate levels of statistical realities: the world of quirky, diverse examples on the one hand, and that of the smooth aggregate on the other. He was, and indeed often continues to be, the answer to a problem encountered by governments, bureaucracies, novelists, and any other body wishing to address and represent a large group, for he represented the "mass"—a large and diverse collection of individuals—in a coherent, easily graspable manner. But what was most remarkable about the synthesis Quetelet intuited was not the nature of Average Man—his ability to combine the general and the particular—but rather the imagining of the solution to this problem in characterological form. Transforming a mathematical formula into a character—one that was, moreover, described as emotionally and politically "balanced"—Quetelet created an imaginary person out of the emotional and characterological possibilities with which, as Desrosières points out, the idea of the average was already invested. For if averages are, as Jevons put it, "numerical results which do not pretend to represent the character of any existing being" (90), they nevertheless project such characters: images of men and women who, widely employed as foundations for governmental policy and marketplace strategy, effectively take on lives of their own, becoming reference points or touchstones not only in the imagining of groups but also in the construction of individual identities.[5] Translating identities into numbers, nineteenth-century statisticians thus also did the opposite, lending their calculations to the creation of a series of figures with whom future identities would have to contend.[6]

The Many in the One

Desrosières argues that the emergence of statistics in the nineteenth century constructed a new object of study—"society"—and hence a new reality. "Realities of superior level [were] capable of circulating as synthetic substitutes for multiple things (*the* price index, for increases in products; *the* unemployment rate, for unemployed persons); emphasis in original."[7] At the same time, each register operates separately: "The various mechanisms have autonomous internal consistency. . . . 'Statistics' (in the sense of the *summary* of a large number of records) often plays an important part in establishing this consistency" (70). Not only is it the case that different registers or realities function distinctly, that is, but individuals and discourses themselves move between registers: it is possible to "circulate effortlessly among several levels of reality, whose modes of construction are nonetheless very different." Transforming diverse elements into what appeared to be a uniform whole—an average—was the business of what Desrosières calls "the magical transmutation of statistical work" (71). The average man is both the result of this magic and a means of perpetuating it: a mechanism by means of which more of the same magic takes place. For what circulates, by means of this fantastically ordinary creature, are elements of character, shuffled and redistributed in such a way that the impersonal "you"—someone (or many "ones") I have never met—becomes a part of "me."[8]

For example: not only did Quetelet posit that individuals contribute to an abstract whole known as society, but he also theorized that each individual contains a portion of that society within him. If in a given society, for instance, some members of the population were deemed likely to commit the crime of robbery, it followed that each member of the general population contained within himself a "penchant" for that particular crime, corresponding in degree to the population of the group as a whole. Thus the average man "could be assigned a 'penchant for crime' equal to the number of criminal acts committed divided by the population" (Porter, *Rise* 53). The effect of such reasoning is evident in nineteenth-century statistical writing, as in the following passage from Henry Mayhew's *London Labour and the London Poor*:

> According to the Criminal Returns of the metropolis . . . labourers occupy a most unenviable pre-eminence in police history. One in every twenty-eight labourers, according to these returns, has a predisposition for simple larceny: the average for the whole population of London is one in every 266 individuals; so that the labourers may be said to be more than 9 times as dishonest as the generality of people resident in the metropolis. In drunkenness they occupy the same prominent position. One in every 22 individuals of the labouring class was charged with being intoxicated in the year 1848; whereas the average number of drunkards in the whole population of London is one in every 113 individuals. Nor are they less pugnaciously inclined; one in every 26 having been charged with a common assault of a more or less

aggravated form. The labourers of London are, therefore, 9 times as dishonest, 5 times as drunken, and 9 times as savage as the rest of the community. (233)

Mayhew and Quetelet do not exactly situate the one "against" the many (to borrow from Alex Woloch—though this is what the trope of "pugnaciousness" suggests); rather, they position the many *in* the one.[9] As the equation has it, the number of "pugnacious" London laborers is greater than the number of pugnacious Londoners; therefore each individual laborer contains a greater "predisposition"—Quetelet's "penchant"—for pugnacity than do members of the general population. But because of the existence of these pugnacious laborers, the average Londoner carries a degree of pugnaciousness within himself as well. The idea of the average entails not only the construction of a new reality, then—a new image of society as a whole—but it also gives rise to the conception of a new kind of individual: one who is imagined as containing society within him or herself. (Indeed, if, in Mayhew's formulation, the pugnacious few represent a threat to the less aggressively disposed many, that threat is resolved here by constructing an individual in thrall to his own pugnaciousness, so that, ultimately, he represents a threat chiefly to himself.)

Or, to put it another way, it is not the case that the "penchant" emerges from a number of individuals, or is understood to emerge in any way from the individual; rather, the individual becomes a function of the mass or the group (wrote Quetelet, "the social state . . . prepares these crimes, and the criminal is merely the instrument to execute them" [6]). Statistics filters out a potentially vast number of individual differences in favor of a smaller collection of similarities, with the result that the idea of the many—*an* idea of the many, constructed by statistics—becomes instrumental in theorizing the nature of the one.[10] Indeed, the many become effectively inseparable from the one, since in this formulation, as in Mayhew's example, the elements out of which statistically meaningful groups are constructed—height, gender, income, class, or other criteria—are assimilated to constructions of individual identity. Knowledge of the individual originates outside the individual; in a crucial sense, the individual may be said to originate outside himself, since what is said to exist within each individual is drawn from some selected, ideologically significant, aspect of the group as a whole. Imagined as a figure in whom the many exist, then, Average Man represents the solution to the problem of imagining a statistical being: he is the one in whom the many may, without contradiction, be perceived. And, increasingly, he is also a figure for the many who inhabit the one, in the form of an imaginary being in relation to whom individual identity is constructed.

Likeness Anxiety

Brought into existence as a fictional being, the average man contributes an increasing fungibility, or likeness, to the imagining of individual identity.[11] In a historical context in which success is figured as an emergence into visibility, the distinction of the self from an otherwise undistinguished mass—the context, that is, of the nineteenth-century novel—the average represents the absorption of identity by that mass. Indeed, in novelistic representation, the average is aligned not only with the balanced ideal, as in Quetelet's formulation, but also with the phenomenon of likeness itself, in the form of characters by means of whose representation the problem of likeness—what might be called likeness anxiety—can be summarily represented and dispatched.[12]

Quetelet's solution to the problem of multiplicity is, as the statue anecdote suggests, an aesthetic one; it is also, significantly for a reading of the Victorian novel, a characterological one.[13] It selects from a great number of people a few qualities; it constructs an imaginary figure who possesses these qualities; it arranges all other individuals around that figure in degrees of likeness and difference. This positioning of characters around a central figure—as deviations from an idealized norm—bears a certain resemblance, as I have suggested, to the Victorian novel, and one novel it resembles strikingly is *Middlemarch:* a novel in which the issue of likeness anxiety takes on tragic proportions, and in which, as in Quetelet's statistics, that anxiety both manifests itself in and is at least provisionally resolved by the construction of a certain kind of character. For the great problem faced by *Middlemarch*'s central characters (as by Eliot herself) is how to *be* a central character: how to avoid being "like" that unenviable body known as "everyone else." And the solution, this formulation suggests, lies in a narrative strategy (both widely employed and widely taken for granted) that consolidates "everyone else" in characterological form.

This strategy epitomizes—to such an extent that it could be said to caricature—the construction of novelistic character per se in the nineteenth century. For since the general project of the nineteenth-century novel is the representation of society, but the "many" are, by definition, too many—impossible to account for empirically—the novel, like statistics, can evoke them only through condensation or encapsulation: by shrinking a multiplicity of individuals into a single entity, or what novel theory usually calls a "type." Thus the "many" are represented as the "one" via the suggestion that any number of individuals are "like" others—so that, having seen one, you might just as well have seen them all. Here, for example, is *Middlemarch*'s description of Mary Garth: "If you want to know *more particularly* how Mary looked, *ten to one* you will see some face like hers in the crowded street tomorrow. . . . If she has a broad face and square brow, well-marked eyebrows and curly dark hair, a certain expression of amusement in her glance which her mouth keeps the secret of, and for the rest features entirely insignificant—take that ordinary but not disagreeable person for a portrait of Mary Garth" (443; my emphasis). Mary is recognizable chiefly because "you" (another condensation) have seen someone (indeed, many) like her before; her face, most of its features deemed "entirely insignificant" (because they are "like" many others), encodes the very tension between the one and the many, the particular and the ordinary, the novel's larger character system fleshes out. Indeed, her face is notable chiefly because it is not only her face: it already belongs, not just to another, but to many others. (And the pressures of statistical likeness extend to the hypothetical reader as well: it may be, for instance, that "you" will see a face like Mary's tomorrow; the chances, says Eliot's narrator, are ten to one that you will. Thus inscribed, the reader is no less a function of statistics than Mary herself: however singular a creature you may feel yourself to be, if you fail to see a person resembling Mary in the street tomorrow you will know that, for every ten who did see her, there is another just as singular as you who did not.)[14] This codification of identity-features positions Eliot's system of characterization alongside Quetelet's: though Eliot would never take the average for an ideal, her method of characterization invokes generalized central figures around whom others are arranged, and in relation to whom any real-life examples—persons a reader might see on the street—are figured as deviations.

Or consider Sir James Chettam, that unsuccessful suitor of Dorothea and successful suitor of Celia for whom the phrase "a fellow like Chettam" serves as descriptive tag, conveying the idea that his most important feature is his similarity to others—those others, it might at this point go without saying, who are also like him. Indeed, it can go without saying that what Chettam's degree of likeness signifies is the undesirability of being a person like himself—a distaste even he has assimilated. When he learns that any proposal of his to Dorothea will be refused, for instance, he refrains from making one, congratulating himself later that "he was not *one of those gentlemen who* languish after the unattainable Sappho's apple that laughs from the topmost bough" (85; my emphasis). Entertaining the possibility of doing something someone like him might be expected to do—proposing "above" himself in the novel's characterological hierarchy—he refuses, and his satisfaction at having repudiated the dictates of his Chettam-like self confirms the correctness of his designated (social and characterological) place. More precisely, his relief is referred to the idea that he has not done what others, in a similar situation, would do: those others who, called into being for the purpose of contrast, serve to represent what he would have done were he foolish enough to actually be someone like himself. In other words, when confronted with the possibility that an action he wishes to take will not be well received, he conjures up an imaginary group of others who would have made that unfortunate choice. The rejected action is then projected onto, or embodied in, this faceless mass, without which he—a fellow like Chettam—would not exist. And his relief at not having done what these newly constructed "others" would have echoes a more widespread condition of avoidance, in which the pursuit of a wished-for identity requires the evocation and disavowal of another presence (discovered within and projected without, but also discovered without and projected within): a someone potentially "like" everyone else—or, if one is already like everyone else, as in the case of Chettam, a someone like oneself, in relation to whom vigilant monitoring and active avoidance are felt to be necessary. "Those gentlemen who"—those "others" Chettam avoids being "one of," who would have made the mistake he avoids making—figure in his identity as a kind of necessary background, a setting from which he (an utterly undistinguished character, in the novel's terms) can then distinguish himself.

But if Chettam himself is only "like" Chettam, what is Chettam like? A pale rendition of Quetelet's Prussian statue, Chettam only exists as a fellow "like" Chettam because, despite his desired separation from others, he represents an entity that possesses more reality than he does: the mass or the group.[15] (Mary Garth's face is, similarly, an imperfect copy of a "mass" face). Indeed, in a world in which "fine young women" contend with "purple-faced bachelors" (120); women in general are either "plain" or "what women ought to be" (121); and even Will Ladislaw (whose idea of genius lies in an "attitude of receptivity towards all sublime chances," which include "too much" wine, lobster, and opium, and whose hair is "not immoderately long, but abundant and curly" [1–9; 219]) might turn out to be "*a* Byron, *a* Chatterton, *a* Churchill—that sort of thing" (107; my emphasis), every "individual" is a copy of a generalized type, and Chettam stands as a *reductio ad absurdum* of the idea that the route to identity lies in a likeness to someone else. Of course, Eliot identifies this perspective as the Middlemarch one: the speakers here are Brooke, and Lydgate in his Middlemarch mode. And yet the ridicule of Chettam—indeed, the character of Chettam, which amounts to the same thing—illustrates the novel's general strategy for dealing with the likeness anxiety Chettam himself represents. For Chettam reproduces, in his disavowal of others, the novel's own strategy for dealing with the possibility that any individual, including oneself, might turn out to be the average man. Representing not a person but many persons—exemplifying the fiction that the many has (indeed, is) a character—Chettam, and with him the intolerable idea of too much likeness, can be managed in a way that those unrepresentable (and otherwise unimaginable) others cannot.

"The world is full of hopeful analogies," writes Eliot (109): images of characters and achievements to be instructively compared with one another. The very idea of imagining the world as a field for the discovery of analogies reflects an averaging mentality, in which individual characters or narratives are significant because they reflect qualities discovered in numerous characters and narratives. In a world thus imagined the many are never very far from the one, and it is for this reason that a mere glance from the wrong young woman at the wrong moment may prove fatal to a young man's ability ever to escape the terrors of an ordinary life:

> In the multitude of middle-aged men who go about their vocations in a daily course determined for them much in the same way as the tie of their cravats, there is always a good number who once meant to shape their own deeds and alter the world a little. The story of their coming to be shapen after the average and fit to be packed by the gross, is hardly ever told even in their consciousness; for perhaps their ardour in generous unpaid toil cooled as imperceptibly as the ardour of other youthful loves, till one day their earlier self walked like a ghost in its old home and made the new furniture ghastly. Nothing in the world more subtle than the process of their gradual change! In the beginning they inhaled it unknowingly; you and I may have sent some of our breath towards infecting them, when we uttered our conforming falsities or drew our silly conclusions: or perhaps it came with the vibrations from a woman's glance. (174)

Imagining a later self as a setting for an earlier one, whose presence "like a ghost in his old home" renders "the new furniture ghastly," Eliot posits a world in which the presence of others within the single individual allows for the perception of many where there had previously been only one. Indeed, the imagining of a single, individual life as a palimpsest, two parts juxtaposed against one another, projects the one as a personification of the many, with an earlier self encountering the fallen, undifferentiated self and transforming it into the unfortunate setting—the ghastly furniture—for its image of earlier ambition. This, in fact, is the novel's way of imagining Lydgate, that character in all of *Middlemarch* who is most actively involved in wrestling with his inner average man, and in whose person the novel's general distinction between the exceptional and the average appears as a drama of two internalized selves.

Lydgate: The Ordinary vs. the Extraordinary

When, in response to an alarm over Mr. Casaubon's health, Lydgate listens to the scholar's heartbeat, he does only what it is the physician's job to do: he checks the sound for regularity and tone, comparing its rhythm to a standard he bears in his mind. One might think that any investigation of Casaubon's heart must be metaphorical: what kind of sound might one expect to issue from such a site, after all, but the rustling of pages, or the shutting of a door? But when the physician examines the patient, realism trumps metaphor, and the heart reveals only the bare truth of the patient's condition. The scene refers, in other words, to a dry, unmetaphorical construct, much like Casaubon himself. Lydgate's performance suggests one reason why the professional medical man may be more attuned to the idea of the average than others: medicine depends upon it. In actual life, of course, there is no such sound and no such consensus (they are averages), but the idea of statistical steadiness suggests both, and Lydgate's character is dominated by such ideas of consensus, and the desires that both issue from and define them.[16]

It is customary to understand Lydgate's character as a pitting of the extraordinary against the common, the latter having infiltrated his consciousness in the form of the "spots of commonness" that compel certain significant, doomed choices: the choice of Rosamond Vincy for his wife; the choice of Tyke over Farebrother. Eliot defines him as possessing "two selves within him": an average or "common" self, on the one hand, and a self seeking escape from the average on the other. Eliot's imagining of Celia as "setting" for Dorothea differs little, in fact, from Lydgate's imagining of Rosamond and her trappings (chief among them bad furniture) as background for his intellectual endeavors. Just as Celia's ordinary desire for jewels provides the initial ground for our understanding of her as an ordinary character in relation to whom the more particular qualities of her sister will appear, so too is Lydgate's relationship with Rosamond Vincy (herself an example of the idealized average, "instructed to the true womanly limit, and not a hair's length beyond" [352]) an expression of his "common" self, the self that "sets off" the famous physician.

Lydgate's identity—made up of a self given over to "others" and a self that hopes to emerge, distinct, from that background—internalizes *Middlemarch*'s foreground/background structure. But the self that exists only against a background is, of course, a self to which background is essential: it is as thoroughly made up of imagined others as the character of Average Man himself. Moreover, his favored identity—the exceptional one that strives against the petty medium of the group—is no less a function of a mass identification than his common one:

> Considering that statistics had not yet embraced a calculation as to the number of ignorant or canting doctors which absolutely must exist in the teeth of all changes, it seemed to Lydgate that a change in the units was the most direct mode of changing the numbers. He meant to be a unit who would make a certain amount of difference towards that spreading change which would one day tell appreciably upon the averages, and in the meantime have the pleasure of making an advantageous difference to the viscera of his own patients. (175)

Imagined not merely as *having* an effect on the whole, but as *being* an effect on the whole, Lydgate's superior self is an effect of the nineteenth-century's statistical context: an identification with a statistically-defined entity. Thus the picture of Lydgate the novel actively encourages—that of a higher sensibility invaded or infected by commonness, by the inevitable internalization of the average—is exposed as a product of wishful thinking: both selves are the function of impersonal structures, derived from ideas of the group.

Indeed, the structure of Lydgate's character is an effect of the same likeness anxiety that marks James Chettam's. Like Chettam, he gains a sense of individual identity by imagining the common man he would rather not be; like Chettam, the self he wishes to claim as his own is no less a function of group identity than the self he rejects. Incorporating the average man along with the exceptional one, but insisting on a barrier between them—"that distinction of mind which belonged to his intellectual ardour, did not penetrate his feeling and judgment about furniture, women, or the desirability of its being known (without his telling) that he was better born than other country surgeons" (179)— Lydgate is an apt model not just for the nineteenth-century physician, or for any other person who refers his or her sense of identity to the idea of an inner average, but for the Victorian-novel reader as well: that figure who, identifying while reading with the process of social aspiration, with movement away from the average, is in the very act of doing so conscripted into a group of others "like" him or herself. This reader, moreover, is not called upon to choose between the average the novel disparages and the individual it valorizes, but is rather invited to identify with both, by means of the structure and process of differentiation (foreground/background) that brings individuality into view. Only such identification could account for the pleasure Eliot's representation of ordinary characters offers its ostensibly ordinary readers, who are invited to indulge a feeling of happy superiority with regard to those *other* others—Brookes, Cadwalladers, Chettams—with whom they are implicitly grouped. For like the characters he or she reads about, the reader is a mass character, the ground for an ungrounded identity: a reference point around which other identities can be arranged and a background from which such identities, not least that of the author herself, can brilliantly emerge. But the persona of Eliot's reader is not exactly relegated to the background: rather, he or she is located somewhere (of course) in the middle, between the comically low Cadwallader and the tragically high Dorothea, the social axis aligned with a temporal one in which the single self plays every role. Thus, as with Lydgate and Dorothea—even, in his own way, Chettam—-the earlier self and the later can be imagined as meeting, the one shedding light on (or serving as background for) the other. The *Middlemarch* reader is, in other words, constructed as a mobile and knowing member of the mass: someone whose reluctance to be assimilated to the group has been fully anticipated.[17]

Trajectories of Feeling

The authorial imagination that defines character in terms of similarity and difference resembles the scientific imagination of nineteenth-century political economist William Stanley Jevons, who sought to adapt Jeremy Bentham's pleasure-pain calculus to commodity culture and

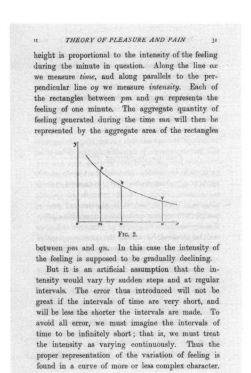

Figure 1. Jevons's emotional intensity graph.

market society. Jevons vivified the pleasure-pain axis by redefining it as the purchase or non-purchase of commodities: what for Bentham were responses to potentially different stimuli were for Jevons wholly identified with consumer behavior (thus for Jevons buying indicates pleasure, and not buying suggests, if not pain, at least an absence of pleasure). Thus transformed, feeling became, for Jevons, measurable: it became a commodity. Measurement renders all emotion equivalent: Jevons positioned feeling on a scale, imagining a continuum from less to more. Indeed, in Jevons's work, the comparative thinking that takes characterological shape in Eliot and Quetelet appears in the form of a graph, substituting smoothness for distinction, "spots" with a single line (figure 1).

Jevons thus renders identity less a matter of clear distinctions than one of graduated differences: differences not of kind but of degree. And not only does this system conceive of pleasure and pain as essentially undifferentiated—varying amounts of the same stuff—but with respect to this axis, Jevons believed, individuals were self-regulating, adjusting their own comfort or discomfort, loss and gain, in a manner that both reflects and governs the larger economic system. "The mind is portrayed as a balance . . . register[ing] both moments of equality and the points at which the balance between two things tips in one direction" (Morgan 242). This image of intuitive balance reproduces in microcosm the images of both individual and group identity on which both nineteenth-century statistics and Eliot's novel rely: it represents character as a homeostatic system, its class-inflected components rising and falling (see epigraph) in relation to their midpoint.

And yet rather than do away with differences in character, as the image of a graduated line suggests, Jevons's trajectory of feeling redefines them, hardening the measurement of feeling into objectifiable characteristics. In the quantifying imagination, quantity replaces quality and eventually becomes it; individuals are characterized less by the nature of the qualities and feelings they possess than by the amount of qualities and feelings they possess. This quantification of feeling is ultimately, of course, about the tracking of commodities and prices, and Jevons's project epitomizes the many gestures toward feeling-measurement with which capitalist society abounds: the widespread acceptance, for instance, of the idea that (in Jevons's words) the "oscillations of the will . . . are minutely registered in the price lists of the markets" (11–12). Situating otherwise undifferentiated individuals on an emotional scale, Jevons's statistical thinking creates a new reality out of which new forms of character emerge.

For the statistical redefinition of character reshapes the representational possibilities for character in the novel, as it does for the identities of readers and nonreaders alike. Thus while it may not be possible to determine *what* others feel, Eliot's narrator, characters, and readers famously assess *how much* feeling they have, attributing to a degree—a relative amount—the quality of an objective reality. And the quantitative difference that makes some characters central and others peripheral is a difference inscribed in and as character. Hence in *Middlemarch,* a character is either a brook or a shallow rill; Chettam is "just the sort of man a woman would like" (63) while Dorothea is "passionate" and "ardent," and the apogee of human consciousness is, in the words of the novel's well-known balancing formulation, the ability to see another as an "equivalent center of self."[18] Making difference from and similarity to others into objective facts about character, Eliot turns quantity into quality. Indeed, given the fungibility of identity in these definitions—the way quantities take shape as qualities—it makes sense that what characterizes Dorothea most of all is a quantity transformed into a quality, and not incidentally that quality Jevons termed feeling's only "inherent" dimension: "intensity."[19]

In contrast to Mary Garth, recognizable because of her resemblance to others, Dorothea's most admirable quality is that there is nobody like her. "It seemed as if she had taken a vow to be different from all other women," notes Eliot's narrator; "Mrs. Casaubon is too unlike other women for them to be compared with her," claims Will Ladislaw (474). The pressure to be different manifests itself as what Eliot calls "extreme" behavior, as in Dorothea's response to the flattering but inconvenient detail that Sir James seems to be "very much in love with her": "The revulsion was so strong and painful in Dorothea's mind that the tears welled up and flowed abundantly" (59). It defines her inability to communicate to her sister the nature of her feeling about Casaubon: "You would have to feel with me," she says, referring in her defense to nothing other than the absence of any possible likeness between her sister's feeling and her own.

What defines Dorothea's character, like Lydgate's, that is, is not just the fact of her difference from others, but the novel's persistent engagement with the issue of that difference. The pressure exerted on character by the idea of difference points less toward a secure opposition (between, for instance, a "one" and a "many") than toward an image of characters as elements in a graduated scale, each only several degrees away from any other, with an effect of individuality made possible only through the gaining of a subjectively-determined secure degree of distance from those with whom one might otherwise tend to merge (an amount—like the judgment of "equivalence"—experienced as large enough to be considered substantive, to undergo the transformation from feeling to object). For if what one knows to be important about Dorothea is that there is no one like her, then a relationship—hers to the group of which she is a part—has been transformed into a fact: indeed, the crucial fact about her identity. Identity thus inheres in the absence of the likeness that characterizes others, and that emerges in the nineteenth century as the defining feature of the mass and its representatives. Just as in the nineteenth-century novel in general it is impossible not to encounter "a" Miss Bates, "a" Mrs. Cadwallader, or "a" James Chettam—characters whose signal function is to evoke the specter of others "like" themselves—so too is nineteenth-century novelistic character often concerned with the need to attend to, contend with, and even occasionally embrace the average within.

Like Jevons, Eliot identifies commonness with desire: Lydgate's common self is the self that cares about furniture, the self that desires Rosamond for her knowledge of and similarity to commodities. The common self is the consumer self, wanting what others want. It is for this reason that the story of Lydgate's downfall is a love story, and more specifically a story about a failed romance with an idealized average. Choosing a wife based on an image of the accoutrements someone "like" him would require—one who provides the background (and balance) for his "other" self, the self that is to do great things—Lydgate's desire, like Rosamond's, is a desire referred to an ideal of balance, even to the point of avoiding "long courtships" and "late marriages" (387). It is a desire based on the apparent absence of idiosyncracy or eccentricity, the quirkiness that, in nineteenth-century fiction in general, might be said to stand in place of a more substantively-felt (and less easily represented) individuality: on Rosamond as the apparent incarnation of "perfect womanhood" (387) and Lydgate's sense of his own "perfect" dress and "perfect" behavior (382), in a world in which such things—the perfect wife, the right furniture—come to signify one's degree of happiness (in fact, Jevons invented a word for those things one did not like and thus would not buy: aptly linking the idea of discomfort with that of the commodity, he called them "discommodities"). And the necessity of a background for the self, along with the novel's ambivalent attitude toward those who are said to embody it (including, of course, the novel's readers) is inscribed in the plot of Lydgate's romance: the falling in love with the "ordinary" self so that one's secret hatred of it, one's disillusionment with it—one's desire not to be, of all selves, *that* one—can be expressed. But my point is not to account for the novel's failed marriages, but rather to note the relentlessly comparative context for the choices its characters make. For if Lydgate's marriage fulfills each partner's sense of what "everyone" would want, that of Dorothea and Will is based on the conviction (shared by readers as well) that neither character is like anyone else.

In a world drenched in statistical thinking and informed in numerous ways by the idea of the average, *Middlemarch* positions its readers within a consciousness whose cognitive mode is relentlessly comparative, in which character emerges as a closeness to or distance from an average. Through the pressure of narratorial evaluation and comparison, that is, Eliot offers less a representation of the average man than a projection of character as an awareness of his inescapability. Thus despite the novel's insistence on ventriloquizing the "middle" perspective—the displacement onto characters such as Brooke and Cadwallader of a "Middlemarch" attitude, in which Chettam is "the kind of man a woman would like," and Rosamond the perfect type of the marriageable woman—*Middlemarch* itself is shaped at every level by the idea of comparison: from its title, to its "Three Love Stories" structure, to the observation that the gray Casaubon appears even grayer when standing next to Ladislaw, to the multiple points of view and equivalent centers of self on which it famously insists. In the context of the incessant measurement and comparison that inform the narrator's accounts of characters and their own of themselves, the desire to be "another" Milton, Bichat, or St. Theresa signifies less an admiration for the particularity of these figures, the specificity of their accomplishments, than a paradoxical desire to imitate individuality per se, as if only thus is it possible to avoid what appears—by contrast, of course—to be a more ordinary kind of likeness. Such appeals normalize or naturalize the very condition the novel rails against: the impossibility, in a world in which "real" identity is mass identity, of not orienting oneself in relation to it, and not identifying in some sense with it.

CHAPTER TWO

Cardiac Excitability

Impulse, Restraint, and "the Pulse
of the People"

In popular discourse, the stock market has long held the status of a force of nature: "Like the ocean," wrote Philip Carret in 1930, "the stock market is never still" (xv). It is assumed to follow the law of gravity—"what goes up must come down"—as well as the psychological equivalent of that law, which dictates that those who have profited from their involvement in the market, especially those who have profited a great deal, must eventually see their winnings disappear. Like nature but with more personality, the market is said to have good days and bad ones: to be up or down; excited or depressed; optimistic or pessimistic. It is liable to sudden, unpredictable mood swings, usually ascribed to the actions of speculators, who upset what would otherwise be—or so this narrative has it—a regular and healthy constitution. It is granted independent agency, sometimes "act[ing] as if there were better things in sight" (Train 92); it makes choices: "When there are two main pressures, one favorable and one unfavorable, the stock market . . . will usually at different times discount each alternative" (83). Generally, the stock market is understood to reflect the actions of a group of disparate individuals collectively known as investors, whose purchases and sales of shares and securities are commonly described in the language of emotion. On any particular day, for instance, "investors" may be described as (for instance) confident, hesitant, gloomy, or optimistic. Such formulations resolve the diverse and innumerable motives behind diverse and innumerable transactions into uniform narratives that purport to explain the differences between one day's (or week's, or year's) stock prices and another's. And they assimilate what would otherwise be a bewildering collection of numbers to a repertoire of emotional states or psychological conditions which extend, because of the market's national and now global significance—and because of the extent to which ordinary (or average) citizens are, either deliberately or unwittingly, "in" the market—beyond specific investors to encompass, to varying degrees, the nation and the world. In stock-market discourse, by way of the representation of the "average" investor's emotional trajectory, the individual becomes the group and the group becomes the individual. "If the stock market were a patient of mine," writes one popular analyst—himself the inventor of something called BMDS, or Bear Market Depressive Syndrome—"I would call him manic depressive" (Schott 147).

Georg Simmel has observed that money lacks the regulation human capacity imposes on concrete objects; money, he writes, "has no inherent or external reasons for restraint" (183–84). There is perhaps no better image for the issues of control posed by money, and the narratives by means of which those issues are addressed, than the stock market—or better yet, the figure by which it is commonly known, the wavering line of the stock-market graph—a line whose peaks and troughs are scrutinized, as Robert Shiller writes, "like tea leaves": yoked to narratives that purport to explain what the market is doing (xiv). Indeed, the stock market tends to attract the kind of magical thinking that surrounds other events perceived as being outside human control (think of a rain dance). Thus "investors" and their range of familiar behaviors and feelings; thus the existence and endurance of the genre of investment-advice manuals. During the "boom" period of the 1990s these manuals proliferated, recounting the experiences of investors such as Warren Buffett and George Soros so that readers could learn to do as they did. These "Money Masters," as one author dubs them, seek out investments no one else knows about, "short" what everyone else is bullish on, or—in a bit of advice whose practical uselessness captures the genre's magical quality—buy "when things are bad, but just about to get better—not when they already are getting better" (Train 24). One broker pays close attention to what "the 48 year-olds" are doing; others advise clients to trust their gut feelings, or "inner investor" (Schott 10). All of these ideas and more—claims for stock tips or insider information, elaborate parsings of the words of Alan Greenspan or the current Chairman of the Federal Reserve—sustain the widespread belief that a key to understanding the stock market exists and can, with some effort, be uncovered. The genre of stock-market advice, in effect, constitutes a collective denial of the possibility that the market may conform to no decipherable logic and be subject to no controlling authority: that there may be no narrative at all in the stock-market graph.

Internalization

While advice manuals from the nineteenth century to the twenty-first offer suggestions about what kind of investments an ordinary person should make, contemporary (twentieth and twenty-first century) popular manuals tend to focus more on self-control: the investor's need to control his or her emotions. As in a relationship in which one partner is subject to sudden, inexplicable mood changes, the task of the co-dependent is said to be separation, the key to successful investing is to resist identifying, or, in the genre's terminology, "overidentifying" with one's investments—a condition characterized by the thought, "this stock is me" (Schott 14). The task of the individual investor is to "master" him- or herself (18), refusing the constant emotional upheavals each day's prices would bring if one took them personally—refusing to allow the market to define one as a loser or a winner. This, of course, is what one is doing anyway. But (the argument goes) if you can train yourself to wait long enough, you will necessarily win, since bad news will eventually turn into good: "It's only a matter of setting out on that slow, sure path that, over time, can bring you the riches you deserve" (38).

Formulated in this way, investment resembles less what it seems most to resemble—gambling—and more what it seems least to resemble: hard work. And the work required is emotional labor, of the sort required by a spiritual or religious discipline.[1] If one succeeds in this discipline, developing what the books call a "winning investor personality," there is no possibility of disappointment, since the good news one is waiting for is always just around the corner and its failure to materialize nothing more than a sign that it is still on the way: "Over time, and with patience, you will emerge from investing a financial winner. This knowledge is a powerful antidote to the down times you may experience" (35). Not for nothing, then, does American Funds' *Investor* Magazine—a leaflet published by a mutual funds' group—tell the story of thirty-eight Benedictine nuns of the Sacred Heart Monastery in western North Dakota, who, having cast their lot with American Funds rather than government securities, "had to learn to live with the ups and downs of equity markets." Says Sister Paula, "'I felt a little flutter in my heart when I saw that one of our accounts lost $50,000 on paper one month and then gained it back the next month.' Several sessions with the order's financial advisers helped the nuns keep an even keel during market downturns" (6). The work this anecdote describes is emotional: the management not of funds, but rather of its investors' feelings—the task, in effect, to transform what feels like speculation (a flutter in the heart) into what feels like investment, without any alteration in the activity itself. Focusing not on the transaction but on its accompanying emotions, advisers seek to distract Sister Paula from attending to the fund whose expansions and contractions her heart, when she does pay attention, instinctively echoes. Labor takes the form of maintaining a nonfluttering heart, staying on an even keel: having faith, so as to ignore the numbers as they change from moment to moment and from day to day.

If the last thing the sisters of the Sacred Heart might perceive themselves as doing is taking a flutter on the market—speculating or gambling—the movement of Sister Paula's heart suggests otherwise: momentarily rupturing the safe distinction between investment and speculation that distances ordinary investors from dramatic market shifts and the uncertainty (and moral taint) of activity defined as speculative, her involuntary response reflects the relation between emotional, physiological, and economic systems that has come to constitute the stock market. More specifically, her response takes shape within a popular narrative of the stock market that, from the Victorian period to the present, has mediated the construction of identities in market society. Within this narrative, the movement of stock prices—and not only for those who speculate or invest—is linked not only to emotion but also to character, by way of those bodily functions most frequently associated with emotion because least susceptible to direct control: the heart and the pulse.

Stock-exchange rhetoric from the nineteenth century to the present has elaborated a narrative that not only represents the market as a character, subject to cyclical bouts of overindulgence followed by necessary corrections, but also emphasizes the presence of that same dynamic in those who attend to it. If nineteenth-century financial advice, as Mary Poovey writes, encouraged readers "to think of finance as the most significant component of the economy and to consider themselves primarily investors or capitalists" (*Financial System* 30), distinctions between impulsiveness and restraint and investors and speculators function similarly, assigning different kinds of financial activities to distinct kinds of characters. Metaphorically linking the movement of stock prices to the emotional condition of stock-market subjects, representations of the market from the Victorian period to the present (including novels, financial journalism, self-help materials, and graphic images) tie the stock exchange, later the stock market, to the visceral responses of hearts and pulses—responses whose inaccessibility to conscious control points toward the truth value of both. The body's apparent echo of market rhythms, that is, suggests the inscription within the self—at the deepest level of character—of a collective narrative that is also everyone's personal story. And the construction of character around the speculation/investment distinction renders the unpredictable and incomprehensible stock market understandable: indeed, and perhaps most crucially, as a shorthand for uncontrolled behavior speculation provides a psychologically and ideologically coherent explanation for the market's inevitable crises.[2]

Because of the link between speculation and an out-of-control market, the route to successful investment, financial advice often suggests, is said to lie in the control of individual emotion: in self-mastery; patience, and detachment from the market's day-to-day fluctuations. Victorian investment advice tended to address external matters, emphasizing the need for safety and minimizing risk: William Wallace Duncan suggests investing only in companies "with over £100,000 capital"; Robert Lucas Nash recommends the three per cents as "the safest investments in the world," and the "Railway investment guide" offers advice in dealing with one's broker, suggesting that one give him "a discretionary range, naming a limit . . . regulated by your own judgment." Twentieth- and twenty-first century advice explicitly counsels patience and emotional restraint, including the idea that the investor should resist identifying with his stocks (Duncan 25; Nash 213; Schott 14, 38). But familiar Victorian lessons about self control were made relevant to the business of trading stocks and shares not chiefly by this kind of financial advice, but rather by the mutually-reinforcing discourses of the novel and the stock exchange, which tie specific kinds of financial activities to distinctions in emotion and character. In a circular system that reinforces an emotional dynamic so familiar as to appear, even now, beyond analysis, novels such as *Little Dorrit* and *The Prime Minister* articulate the underlying psychological features of emotional distinctions on which the stock exchange relies, while financial crises provided grist for the novelistic mill precisely because their strategies of representation—in which, for instance, larger-than-life characters such as George Hudson, the railway king, take the fall for the workings of an impersonal economic system—were already novelistic. The projection of the market as a character, mediated by the Victorian novel, creates a narrative in which all characters—and potentially all readers—are either speculators or investors: not just in the market but in other areas of experience as well. Speculation and investment, that is, provide the terms for a distant reading of the self in a narrative that parallels, even as it is supposed to explain, the workings of the stock market.

Character and the Market

Members of stock-exchange or stock-market societies, whether active investors or not, are positioned "in" the market—in the nineteenth century, by financial journalism that began in the 1820s to address the public as a whole; in the twentieth and twenty-first, by the universal circulation of market stories; the ubiquitous image of the Times-Square ticker tape or stock-market "crawls" on television or computer screens; the graphs and tables that appear daily on those same screens and in newspapers.[3] These phenomena rely on the idea that the state of the market reflects what I argue it produces: an image in which the emotional and economic life of the individual are tied together in a trajectory that also figures the individual's assimilation to the group. The cultural emphasis on the stock market as a continuing emotional drama—what might be called, following Ann Cvetkovich, its sensationalization—establishes a visceral link between the moods of the stock market and those whose emotional and material well-being is rhetorically and imagistically tied to it.[4] The story of how this came to be—how the market came to inhabit the individual, even as the individual inhabits the market—begins with the consolidation of the London Stock Exchange.

Wrote the journalist John Francis in 1850:

> Capel Court is, indeed, a complete anomaly. There are men of high character and station in its body; there is every endeavour made by its executive to abolish all which tends to make it despicable; the greatness of its dealings are unequalled; some of its members are members of the senate; others are honorable in spite of the temptations which surround them; it is consulted by chancellors, and taken into the counsellors of ministers; peace or war hangs upon its fiat; and yet the Stock Exchange is seldom named, out of the city, but with contempt; and a Stock Exchange man is, like the moneyed man in the early reign of William, despised by the landed, and looked down upon by the mercantile, aristocracy. One reason, perhaps, for this is, that the great mass of their transactions are outside the pale of the law. All their time bargains—and the Stock Exchange might close to-morrow if these were abolished—are illegal. They are, strictly speaking, gambling dealings, which our judicature refuses to recognize; and the dealers are gamblers, whom the legislature will not acknowledge. (121)

Between the seventeenth and nineteenth centuries, the buying and selling of stocks and securities grew from a series of activities largely considered disreputable into an institution—still largely considered disreputable—that was nevertheless also perceived as indispensable; it was, in Francis's words, "the theatre of the most extensive money transactions in the world" (121). "A body growing out of small beginnings in speculation, to a height that has given it the command of this nation—its destinies—its ministers of government—its resources—its morals—its private property," it became, and remains today, a semi-sacred space (45). But as Francis's remarks suggest, the exchange did not achieve this status by attaining legitimacy; rather, it did so by articulating a powerful cultural narrative in which feelings, bodies, and money intertwine, and in which the exchange's own perceived relation to the illegitimate, or what takes place "without the pale of the law," plays a crucial role.

The power and status of the early exchange depended upon its securing a specific location. In the late seventeenth century trading took place at coffee houses—chief among them one called Jonathan's—and buyers and sellers moved between different sites, their movement sometimes occasioned by crowding. Indeed, trading momentarily moved outdoors, to a series of streets called 'Change Alley, not far from Jonathan's and the Bank of England. But an indoor location became necessary, for as these moves continued signs of institutionalization appeared in the form of a desire for exclusivity: subscriptions limited the number of people who could participate, and soon the exchange had the quality of a semi-exclusive club. In 1761 such a club was formed, based at Jonathan's, and in 1773 a new site opened with "The Stock Exchange" written over the door (Hennessy 15–16).

From its earliest period, the stock exchange sought to establish its own legitimacy by distinguishing between acceptable and unacceptable forms of trading. Brokering, for instance—acting as an intermediary in a stock transaction—was distinguished from jobbing, in which the trader acted for himself, and the licensing of brokers in 1697, limiting their number to 100, was only one of a series of attempts to establish a formal difference between the activities conducted in the exchange. There was particular anxiety about a process called "dealing for time," the buying and selling of shares with a promise of future payment, since, Ranald Michie writes, "if one or more members failed, owing a large amount of either securities or money to other members, this could produce a chain reaction of collapses, to the detriment of all" (50). Though members sometimes called for the banning of options, this was never done, nor could it be—since options, as many have pointed out, constituted the major—if "unrecognized," as Michie puts it—type of business engaged upon in the market: "unrecognized" because recognition would involve acknowledging that the entire business depended on and, indeed was, a version of what took place "outside the pale of the law."[5] Like speculation, the more familiar term for such activity, jobbing was described as a threat to the institution itself, even though without it, as Francis noted, there would be no exchange at all.

If jobbing was so disliked and so risky, why was it not declared illegal? Francis provides one answer: the entire exchange existed "outside the pale of the law." Because of this, it had to establish rules where none had previously existed; in particular, it had to devise a way to surround with an aura of legitimacy a series of activities that looked to most observers like a form of gambling. On the one hand, much of the exchange's activity was illegal. On the other, the government was becoming increasingly dependent on investors as a source of income; indeed, the Napoleonic Wars could not be fought without them. It was necessary, in other words, for the public to place its trust in an institution and a business never associated with trustworthiness. Writes one historian, "It was not enough for the securities market to develop in terms of intermediation and technique in the eighteenth century. Also required was a system of control which guaranteed that sales and purchases would be honored when they became due. This could not be done in law as Barnard's Act, passed in 1734, had made time bargains illegal, regarding them as a form of gambling. It was thus left to the market participants themselves to create a code of conduct that enforced the conditions necessary for trade" (Hennessy 30–31). But a code of conduct (which included rules against letting off fireworks, knocking off hats, bursting bags of sawdust or flour over the heads of those looking at the subscription lists, and setting fire to coattails and newspapers) was not enough to bestow an effect of solidity on market transactions. Rather, that effect depended on the effort to establish a difference between legitimate and illegitimate forms of trading: a formulation instrumental to the exchange's institutionalization and continued power.

The establishment of the Stock Subscription Room in 1801, the closest precursor of the modern stock market, significantly altered the nature of trading: not just by limiting membership—that had already been done—but by the means through which it did so. As Michie explains, "By controlling admission, introducing full-time administration, and enforcing rules and regulations, they [the members] . . . formed an institution that was far more than the collective actions of those who traded in securities. . . . Essentially, the emergence of a closed market in securities, and all that involved, represented both an end to one evolutionary process . . . and the beginning of another, that now included the control, distribution, and exercise of power and authority. Henceforth, the securities market was no longer an open one which participants could enter at will and act in without redress. Instead, it incorporated not only an enforceable code for business behaviour but also an institutional organization that demarcated member from non-member." And, crucially, "From the outset the Stock Exchange sought to control the admission of members, not so much in terms of absolute numbers but more with respect to type and character" (36–38).[6] Jobbers were permitted in the Stock Subscription Room; indeed, their willingness to buy and sell rapidly was crucial to its flourishing. Other groups, however, such as bill-brokers, bankers, and merchants were excluded. But the relevant point is not that a specific form of trading or kind of trader was always excluded from the exchange, nor that the members of 1801 figured out how to bar the criminals from the door, nor that they succeeded in establishing a clear distinction between legitimate and illegitimate trading. For what mattered was not who was in and who was out, but the insistence that it was possible—imperative, in fact—to distinguish good forms of trading, and good traders, from bad ones.

Thus the stock exchange, which began life outside the boundaries of the law and whose business may accurately be described as the taking of risks with other people's money, sought from its beginnings to establish its security, safety, and respectability by declaring some forms of trading and some kinds of traders to be inadmissable on the basis of illegitimacy or risk. The rhetoric of the 1801 exchange broadened and deepened those distinctions, attaching them, as so many other aspects of Victorian life were attached, to distinctions in character, and soon established members were required to supply references assuring the trustworthiness of new ones. Emphasizing the control of membership "with respect to type and character," then, the exchange's new rules codified assumptions about the relationship between character and specific kinds of financial activities. Distinctions not always clear or indeed relevant to the general public, such as those between bill-brokers, stock-jobbers, and various kinds of merchants and bankers were subsumed within categories that, designating different activities, came to signify differences in character as well.

This new emphasis on character enabled the exchange to extend its influence beyond its own physical boundaries—despite and indeed because of their increased significance. Regulation within the exchange, then as now, was neither completely attainable nor completely desirable: one wants to let the jobbers in, after all. Nor was it necessary, since the

CARDIAC EXCITABILITY / 51

flexible set of determinations about what kinds of traders were admissible and what kind were not already existed alongside a set of assumptions about the relationship between certain kinds of stock-exchange activities and certain kinds of character. Promulgating the idea that the stock exchange was essentially about character, the new exchange buried the shifting requirements of its daily business under a simplified opposition within which members of the general public were invited to position themselves. With the assistance of the financial pages, which in 1825 began publishing daily accounts of stock-exchange activity, and of novels, which made ample use of the perceived relation between certain kinds of business dealings and certain kinds of characters, the world (and not just that of the stock exchange) was divided up into two kinds of people, and it was generally known—without anyone knowing exactly how he or she came to know it—what each kind of person was like. Thus it is well known that an investor is respectable, and has, in addition to his investments, a solid job or career, while a speculator's sole interest is making money into more money. It is known that the investor believes in his investments, and invests for the good of the nation, while the speculator is uninterested in the nature of the company or commodity he buys and sells. The investor is a solid, trustworthy type, the speculator false and deceitful; the investor is patient and weighs his decisions carefully while the speculator acts on impulse. It is known that the investor keeps his emotions on an even keel, maintaining a distance from his money, while the speculator is always watching his money, is too close to his money, is too, well, excited by his money. And it is certainly known of the speculator, not least from Victorian novels, that you wouldn't want your daughter to marry one.[7]

The Pulse of the People

The power of the nineteenth-century stock exchange was closely linked to its exclusivity: to the way in which, in Francis's words, it "conducts all these vast relations with closed doors in a building of its own, and to the entire exclusion of all most materially concerned" (121). This seclusion contributed, as well, to its legitimation: the untrustworthy, or so the story went, could be kept out. But the construction of the stock exchange also connects it metaphorically and viscerally with the human heart: metaphorically, because, like the heart, it is represented as a center out of which vital information flows; viscerally, because the measured release of crucial information from such a source contributes not to the maintenance of investorly calm but rather to the accelerated pulse, the cardiac excitability, on which stock-market culture depends and by means of which it commands attention.

Wrote Charles MacKay in 1841:

M. de Chirac, a celebrated physician, had bought stock at an unlucky period, and was very anxious to sell out. Stock, however, continued to fall for two or three days, much to his alarm. His mind was filled with the subject, when he was suddenly called upon to attend a lady who imagined herself unwell. He arrived, was shewn upstairs, and felt the lady's pulse. "It falls! It falls! Good God, it falls continually!" Said he musingly, while the lady looked up in his face all anxiety for his opinion. "Oh, M. de Chirac," said she, starting to her feet and ringing the bell for assistance; "I am dying! I am dying! it falls! it falls! it falls!" "What falls?" inquired the doctor in amazement. "My pulse! My pulse!" Said the lady; "I must be dying." "Calm your apprehensions, my dear Madam," said M. de Chirac; "I was speaking of the stocks. The truth is, I have been a great loser, and my mind is so disturbed, I hardly know what I have been saying." (20)

Despite their mutual misunderstanding, the doctor and his patient have both got it metaphorically right: the patient, who mistakenly identifies herself as the object of her physician's professional attention, and the physician, whose urgency gives voice to the well-known association between one's money and one's life—in this case, his money and his life, an equation within the parameters of which the spectacle of his own rise and fall is understandably more compelling than his patient's. As he "musingly" takes the woman's pulse, the potential for its fall or (perhaps just the search for a regular rhythm) conjures up another such image, the activity of "taking" perhaps recalling that of "checking," as in the checking of stock prices. Playing the roles of both physician and patient—momentarily attending to and participating in the larger, collective body to which he belongs, the body of investors—the doctor imagines himself unwell as he focuses obsessively on its pulse, his pulse. His hand on the pulse but his mind on the market, he embodies the fantasy of unmediated access that underlies the stock-market-as-pulse metaphor, his signature gesture underscoring the way both physician and stockbroker owe their authority to their imagined contact with some originary, life-giving source. The heartbeat was in 1887 reproduced via electrical impulses as a wavy line on paper (inscribed by a metal pen, as if written by the heart itself); stock prices, understood as indicators of feeling from the exchange's earliest period, were in the 1870's transmitted from source to paper by that newly-invented and suggestively-named recording device, the ticker. Both devices addressed a perceived need, in their separate areas, for precise monitoring; both offered, in strikingly similar visual signs, new opportunities for interpretation. And both were perceived as carrying vital information about the life and health of the individual and the group to which he or she belonged.

The stock exchange has long been a site from which numbers have emanated. John Castaing's *The Course of the Exchange and other things*, published twice weekly in 1698, is said to be "the first in an unbroken succession of published share prices culminating in the *Daily Official List*" (Hennessy 6). Such publication may be required in order to convey information, but it serves another purpose as well, functioning as an advertisement for itself: the price list, like the leap of a fishing lure, possesses the attraction of sheer movement. In the eighteenth century, when available cash would most likely have been invested in land or property, the market in securities had first of all to signal its own existence, and the fluctuation of the numbers indicated the existence of a practice of buying and selling. It drew attention, bringing in new participants.[8]

With the increasing popularity of stock trading in the early nineteenth century, the meaning of the numbers shifted: no longer signifying only their own movement, they became identified with its possible causes as well. As such, they both incited movement in, and became a record of, public feeling: a visible manifestation of what then as now was referred to as "the pulse of the people." Perhaps the most notorious example of the role this newly measurable feeling played in the life of a nation is the way the stock exchange functioned during the Napoleonic Wars, when the rise and fall of prices gauged not what people knew about how the war was going, but rather how people reacted to what they thought stock prices communicated about how the war was going. For instance, "Military success would suggest an end to war and thus a fall in government borrowing, lower inflation, and a decline in interest rates. These factors would drive the price of stocks up. Conversely, defeat would suggest a prolonging of the conflict, and the costs attached to it, which would push prices down. Thus, when a group spread a false rumour on the Stock Exchange in 1814, purporting to come from France and announcing that Napoleon was dead and Paris captured, the price of government stock rose, allowing the perpetrators to make a profit of £10,450 by selling the securities they had bought shortly before" (Michie 51). Markets and exchanges, of course, require no grounding in real-world events in order to respond to them: indeed, in the *mise-en-abyme* the exchange then revealed itself to be, the rise and fall of prices came to signify not how people felt about the war or the nation, but rather how they felt about the stock exchange. Wrote Francis: "The pulse of the people was feverish, and easily excited; and the papers of the day display the intense anxiety which hung over the public mind during the eventful years of 1814 and 1815. It is scarcely an exaggeration to say, that they were regarded as an oracle; and while the public professed to disbelieve all Stock Exchange rumors, simply because they were so, they continued to inquire the variations in the price, and almost regarded them as a cause rather than a consequence. The annals of the world contain no more exciting period" (79). By the nineteenth century, "excitability" had become the name of a cardiac function, and stock prices functioned then, as they do today, as a national EKG. Understood as a visualization of the market, and therefore of "public feeling," stock prices dissolve individual emotion into a larger social body (of the market's own making); they then re-present that emotion to the public, which checks them—takes its own pulse—to discover how it is feeling. The stock exchange, and later the stock market, soliciting identification with the movement of stock prices, grants the collective social body a power and influence beyond any individual's capacity. But what ties that social body—the body made up of those imaginary investors we met earlier—to the individual body, that of the potential or actual investor? In a market economy, the ultimate signifier—always changing, always requiring interpretation—is price. And the perceived importance and unpredictability of the movement of prices yokes that movement, metaphorically and viscerally, to those bodily signifiers—the heart and the pulse—conceived of in the same way: as the center of a vital system and yet beyond any individual's control.

Life and Money Both

The Victorian novel played a major role in aligning specific forms of money-making with specific character types, and by the mid-nineteenth century novelists had added speculation to the list of unsavory qualities a villain could be expected to possess.[9] But the case against speculation is secured not primarily by the predominance of evil speculator characters in novels, but rather by a general, culturally disseminated insistence on an opposition between the qualities speculators are typically said to possess—greed, impatience, and impulsiveness—and investor-like qualities such as patience and self-denial. Tying emotion and character to the stock market, Victorian novels drew upon and reinforced connections made in stock-market rhetoric, primarily by insisting on differences along what may also be seen as an undifferentiated trajectory of feeling. And the establishing of links between character types and modes of doing business was routed, again, through the association between the stock market and the heart.

In Charles Dickens's *Little Dorrit*, the category of self-restraint provides a spectrum across which characters are arrayed, from William Dorrit's famous loss of self-control at an Italian dinner table to his daughter's general, but not complete, composure, to the momentary recklessness that takes the form of speculating on Merdle which lands Arthur Clennam, otherwise a model of restraint, in the Marshalsea prison. Mapped across the novel's population, the ability to restrain the self functions, as it did generally in Victorian culture, as a semic code: a way of establishing differences between characters. And yet in *Little Dorrit* almost every character gives in at some point to the same impulse, suspending the capacity for self-restraint long enough to do what Clennam does: to put some money on Merdle.

After her family has been released from debtors' prison, when she learns that her father will, despite his many years of imprisonment, have to pay his financial debts, Amy Dorrit has one of those rare moments at which what the novel calls "the prison taint" asserts itself, and she complains: "It seems . . . hard that he [her father] should pay in life and money both" (353). Life and money both: the story behind the story of *Little Dorrit* is a tale of lack of restraint in another context, that most commonly associated with the Victorians. But the pervading metonym for lack of restraint in *Little Dorrit* is not the inability to control one's sexuality, but the inability to control one's money. The narrative of sexual transgression is the domestic equivalent of the financial story that provides the novel's framework; the most important context for the maintenance or loss of self-control in the novel is Merdle's stock fraud. The character issue, in other words—why it is that restraint or its absence matters—is a financial one: the danger of impulsiveness in the domestic sphere is that one might take that impulsiveness to the market.

The Merdle fraud, and indeed the entire stock-exchange context, give the novel a certain real-world energy; Merdle is based on the Victorian "railway king" George Hudson. But the energy the novel gains by invoking the world of the stock exchange and of financial scandals (an appeal to the "bottom line," as in the truth-revealing narrative said to be unearthed when one follows the money trail) obscures the ways in which the stock exchange exists less as a framework for the novel than as a parallel to it. For if the novel refers matters of character to the stock exchange, the stock exchange may be said to rely, for explanations of its doings, on forms of character structured by the Victorian novel. If, that is, the novel bolstered its cultural power by referring to the stock exchange, the stock exchange drew—and continues to draw—its own cultural power from the cultivation of habits of thought on which the Victorian novel relied and which it reinforced. With its panoply of recognizable characters (the investor; the speculator; the great and fraudulent financier) and the familiar plots that accompany them, the stock exchange is no less novelistic than the novel itself; indeed, it is a serial novel, periodically offering up a string of scandalous revelations whose most surprising quality could be, though it never is, how little they have changed in two hundred years. The relation between the stock market and the novel recalls Pancks's account, in response to Arthur Clennam's question about who referred Little Dorrit to his mother, of what it means for one person to serve as a "reference" for another:

> "As to being a reference," said Pancks, "you know in a general way, what being a reference means. It's all your eye, that is! Look at your tenants down the Yard here. They'd all be references for one another, if you'd let 'em. What would be the good of letting 'em? It's no satisfaction to be done by two men instead of one. One's enough. A person who can't pay, gets another person who can't pay, to guarantee that he can pay. Like a person with two wooden legs, getting another person with two wooden legs, to guarantee that he has got two natural legs. It doesn't make either of them able to do a walking-match." (228)

Though he is referring specifically to bills of exchange, Pancks's description applies as well to the relation between the novel and the stock market, as well as to the internal workings of the stock market itself. For in the absence of any definitive way to determine value (and this becomes an explicit issue with respect to Ferdinand Lopez, in my discussion of *The Prime Minister* in chapter 3), stock prices rise and fall according to what one person thinks another person thinks that company is worth; stock transactions, in other words, are always guaranteed by a person with two wooden legs. (The system of character reference devised by the Stock Subscription Room of 1801 confirmed its own wooden-leggedness by requiring established members to guarantee, to the tune of 3001, the potential losses of those they recommended [Michie 40]). And the term "reference" comes up as well in relation to one of the sources to which I have been referring: John Francis's *Chronicles and Characters of the Stock Exchange*.

Working the boundaries between journalism, sociology, and fiction, Francis announces as his goal not the production of a work "of a financial kind," as in tables or statistics, but rather "a popular narrative of the money power of England" (vi). The juxtaposition between tables and narrative raises the issue of the meaning of the graph: how it is that numbers and tables can be transformed into story. And even as he represents himself as engaged in this task, Frances seeks to enhance the vividness of his narrative by claiming for his book what I have called the energy of the real. But he does so, in a thoroughly paradoxical manner, by asserting that he is merely transcribing a phenomenon that is inherently novelistic. Thus in the midst of a particularly vivid description of what he calls "a scene . . . worthy the pencil of an artist," he announces that the scene has in fact "been appropriated by a novelist as not unworthy his pen." Here is Francis's version:

> With huge pocketbook containing worthless scrip; with crafty countenance and cunning eye; with showy jewelry and threadbare coat; with well-greased locks and unpolished boots; with knavery in every curl of the lip, and villany [*sic*] in every thought of the heart; the stag, as he was afterwards termed, was a prominent portrait in the foreground. Grouped together in one corner might be seen a knot of boys eagerly buying and selling at a profit which bore no comparison to the loss of honesty they each day experienced. . . . In every corner, and in every vacant space, might be seen men eagerly discussing the premium of a new company, the rate of a new loan, the rumored profit of some lucky speculator, the rumored failure of some great financier, or wrangling with savage eagerness over the fate of a shilling. (96–97)

The unnamed novelist's description—not recognizably different from this one—follows. But what might it mean to say that a scene in real life has been "appropriated by" a novelist? Or to refer to actual life as a "scene"? Francis offers the words of the novelist as a kind of backup for his own account, as if a claim for the novelistic quality of the scene requires authorization from an actual novelist. But his point is really that what accounts for the scene's "worthiness" is that it leaves the novelist, as it does Francis, with nothing to do but copy: the cast of characters (the stag, the speculator, the great financier); the proliferation of story, "every

vacant space" stuffed with characters and plot; the use of clothing to signal financial status and moral worth—all, he claims, are "in" the market.
Shifting the wooden-leg question to the relationship between Victorian
fiction and the reality on which it depends, Francis nullifies the possibility of reference altogether, defining as imperceptible and refining out of
existence, some two hundred years before one might have considered it
necessary, the difference between the stock market and the novel.

The failure of self-control that causes so many in *Little Dorrit* to
invest in Merdle is represented in Dickens's novel as involuntary: for
Dickens, speculation is a disease, and those who fall victim to it are not
responsible for having done so. But this is not the novel's only account
of speculation: Clennam blames himself, as well as Pancks, for "yielding
to this fatal mania" (595), and the terms "yield" and "mania" simultaneously blame and exonerate. Certainly, not every character in the novel
yields, and those who do not are full of reproach for those who do. But
given Merdle's shadowy status—this is a man who lurks behind doors,
who refuses food and sociality, "who had sprung from nothing, by no
natural growth or process that any one could account for" (593); and
given the reach of the disaster—the number of lives affected by it, the
apparent impossibility of not having been, in some way, "in Merdle"—
"Numbers of men in every profession and trade would be blighted by
his insolvency; old people who had been in easy circumstances all their
lives would have no place of repentance for their trust in him but the
workhouse; legions of women and children would have their whole
future desolated by the hand of this mighty scoundrel" (593)—given
all this, Merdle begins to look like a personification of every character's
inner speculator: the companion to the inner investor popular discourse
posits as lurking within everyone's breast. It is not only that we are all
investors or speculators, that is, but rather that we are all investors *and*
speculators, the drama of the stock market represented as an internal
one, a conflict between impulses identified with either side. In *Little
Dorrit*'s character system—the system twentieth- and twenty-first century market culture has inherited from the Victorians—investment and
speculation are the terms of a psychic drama: that same drama from
which the stock market draws its emotional power. Thus recast, the
desire to speculate takes shape as an impulse so irresistible as to seem
natural, so that what comes to seem truly unnatural is the not giving
in to it: the quickened pulse that signals the momentary supremacy of
one's inner speculator (like the complaining that reveals Little Dorrit's
susceptibility to "the prison taint," or the fluttering of Sister Paula's
heart) is the weakness that signifies humanity. The accelerated heart

and pulse evoked by the movement of stock prices thus define as mere cover the legitimacy bestowed on stock-exchange activity by such institutions as brokers or the investor's respectability. Granted the authority to reflect—indeed, to reveal—the true state of our emotions; repeatedly making clear its need for regulation, yet always revealing itself, finally, as ungovernable, the stock market commands our attention, and as members of a stock-market culture we cannot help but pay up.

The Skyline and the Graph

In the days immediately following the 2001 attack on the World Trade Center, Americans were asked to perform two metaphorically equivalent activities—to donate blood and to invest in the stock market—both, ostensibly, for the good of the country: to get the economy moving again. The idea of movement has always been crucial to perceptions of the stock market; thus it makes sense that a symbolic flattening of the New York City skyline should be linked, again both metaphorically and practically, with a flattening of the stock-market graph. In fact, the markets did close immediately after the attack, and much attention was focused on getting them moving again. Indeed, the New York skyline emerged almost instantaneously as a version of the graph: the September 16 *New York Times* juxtaposed images of the skyline and the seismograph that recorded the impact of the airplanes on the towers, describing in an accompanying article the buildings themselves in both seismographic and topographical terms, as forms emerging or forced from the earth: "The skyline may look like an exquisite stroke of calligraphy but it is more akin to the jagged mark of a seismograph, which testifies to deeper upheavals and turbulence below. Convulsive changes in property values, staggering building undertakings, colossal bankruptcies, the reciprocal action of destruction and construction: this is the normal metabolism of a healthy and living city" (Lewis, "Skyline"). But the forces that create these forms are not of course those of nature, but rather those of capitalism: shifts in property values shape the "metabolism"—the topography—of the city. And the question of what their movement means itself takes shape as a kind of Rorscharch test, as the cover of November 11, 2001's Sunday *Magazine* suggests (figure 2). (A letter to the magazine some weeks later, from a physician, claimed that the figure was without doubt an EKG, signifying that "the pulse of New York remains vibrant" [Nissenblatt].)

In the context of listing numerous "Bubbles" in which a gullible public hurries to invest (on the order of "extracting silver from lead," and "buying and fitting out ships to suppress pirates" [57]), Charles MacKay offers the following anecdote:

> [T]he most absurd and preposterous of all, and which shewed, more completely than any other, the utter madness of the people, as one started by an unknown adventurer, entitled, *"A company for carrying on an undertaking of great advantage, but nobody to know what it is."* Were not the fact stated by scores of credible witnesses [another example of men with wooden legs standing up for each other], it would be impossible to believe that any person could have been duped by such a project. The man of genius who essayed this bold and successful inroad upon public credulity, merely stated in his prospectus that the required capital was half a million, in five thousand shares of 100*l*. each deposit 2*l*. per share. Each subscriber, paying his deposit, would be entitled to 100*l*. annum per share. How this immense profit was to be obtained, he did not condescend to inform them at that time, but promised that in a month full particulars should be duly announced, and a call made for the remaining 98*l*. of the subscription. Next morning, at nine o'clock, this great man opened an office in Cornhill. Crowds of people beset his door, and when he shut up at three o'clock, he found that no less than one thousand shares had been subscribed for, and the deposits paid. He was thus, in five hours, the winner of 2000*l*. He was philosopher enough to be contented with his venture, and set off the same evening for the Continent. He was never heard of again. (58)

MacKay's purpose is to trace a history of popular delusions, not to explain them; for him speculation is a mania, a delusion to which some succumb because others have. But the image of the graph suggests a possible explanation for the attraction of such ventures, one that might help explain why Mackay's delusional subjects and others put their money in such schemes. In the representations I have been discussing, the graph, with its wavering line, emerges as an image of emotions without a body: a fantastical consensus from which the bodies that contributed to it have been erased. It appears, in fact, as the truth of those bodies: a picture of raw, unmediated data with which stock-market subjects are invited to identify (it is, after all, supposed to be a picture of us). In doing so, we project our emotions onto it: we wrap ourselves around it; we ride it in our minds. The line wants to move, and in response to its call we become the bodies that move it; it needs to be restrained, and taking it inside

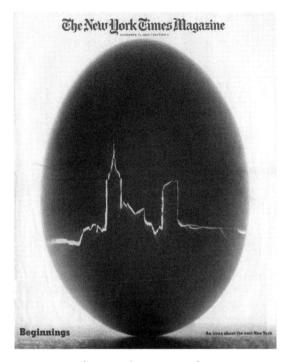

Figure 2. Cover by Raymond Meier, New York Times Magazine, November 11, 2001

ourselves we seek to contain and restrain it. Supporting the graph's illusion of movement and life, we animate it, and it, in turn, animates us.

Postscript

In 2001, researchers connected currency traders to biofeedback machines, measuring their skin temperature, heart rate, and other vital signs as they conducted their business. The resulting image appears as a new kind of EKG, or stock-market graph, merging somatic responses with stock prices, physical symptoms with emotional ones. It is, in effect, a picture of the stock-market graph *as seen through*—and as an image of—the body (figure 3).

Or note the following appeal to scientific authority: a report that the "typical" trader's level of the stress hormone cortisol "fluctuates with the volatility in markets, indicating that it could be a factor in making brokers more cautious during downturns." Enlisting science in the ser-

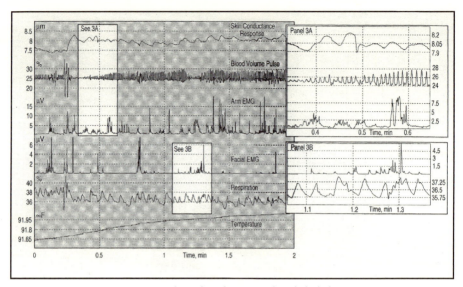

Figure 3. The stock market as seen through the body.

vice of ideology—seeking to ground emotion and stock-market activity in bodily chemistry—these researchers rely on the figure of the "typical trader" they have constructed out of "17 typical London traders—men ages 18 to 38" (Stein). Absent this imagined average trader, with whom each individual trader must somehow be in contact, there would be no narrative, and no certainty—in this case, in the form of a promised biological knowledge—about the way the market works.

CHAPTER THREE

Trollope in the Stock Market
Irrational Exuberance
and *The Prime Minister*

A television advertisement for CNBC, aired frequently before the late-2000 economic decline, features a digital stock ticker projected across the chest of a railway commuter, its numbers coursing around him in a continuous, moving ribbon (figure 4). Like an EKG, or some new kind of medical tracking device, this image—locating the crawl of stock prices where the man's other ticker should be—suggests the quality of contemporary fascination with the stock market by identifying the movement of stock prices with life itself: physical and, especially, emotional life. It evokes the fantasy of connectedness the stock market has become, as its subject is represented as surrounded by—in effect, bound up in—a complex arrangement of digits that must, it seems, signify something crucial about him. Registering both the intensity and the banality of today's incessant market monitoring, the man with the ticker is a new everyman—a more intriguing version of the familiar work-a-day commuter, his internalization of the market (and the admiring gaze of his fellow commuter) singling him out as an enviable type: a vision of how connected we may all someday hope to become. In an age of such heightened attention to stock prices that they can be identified as vital signs, the man with the ticker is our better, more tuned-in, self; watching the numbers, the ad intimates, we are simply watching ourselves.

But how, exactly, are these signs to be read? In both popular and academic discourse, the movement of stock-market prices, especially as represented by the jagged line of the stock-market graph, is amenable both to interpretation and to the failure of interpretation: it looks so much like a narrative, yet no one can say for certain what it means. Or

63

Figure 4. Ticker Man. Courtesy CNBC

rather, everyone has something to say: an encyclopedia of "chart patterns" lists forty-seven variations, with such engaging names as "bump and run reversal," "hanging man," and "dead-cat bounce." The book also includes a chart identifying its own "failure rate": "Percentage of formations that do not work as expected" (Bulkowski 655). A writer on day trading cautions against selling on Mondays, with this caveat: "There is no pattern, relationship, or indicator in the market that will always be correct. . . . Now, getting back to the Monday pattern" (Bernstein 71). Nor does the graph's much-vaunted unpredictability, or "failure rate," disturb such claims; if its trajectory fails to conform to expectations, as it inevitably does, that incoherence is ascribed to the idea that the market knows us better than we know ourselves: more attuned to our desires and fears than any individual human being, it is said to respond to "unpredictable human impulses" (Carret 24). Indeed, most frequently, as the CNBC image suggests, the line's trajectory is assimilated to a narrative of feeling: universally apprehended as a picture of emotions—a snapshot of the national (or global) mood—it is understood to swing (for example) between elation and depression, optimism and alarm. Looking to the numbers to see how we feel, we both personalize them—render them a projection of our individual and collective narratives—and depersonalize them, conceding our authority to know ourselves to an abstract system that seems to have captured this knowledge. Do the numbers emerge from within the man's chest, or are they projected from without? Is the market a projection of the man, or is the man a projection of the market? Making sense of the numbers, we seek to discover, in that familiar phrase that registers the identification of economic with emotional well-being, how we are doing.

The market must have some authority of its own, it seems—it can't be just us, writ large—and yet it appears to be. The idea of the stock market as emotional projection bears on the question, addressed by market theorists, of whether stock prices are determined by facts about companies or commodities (that is, by how they are doing), or by the activity of investment. The contention that stocks in the dot-com economy of the 1990s were overvalued was tied to an assessment of investor emotion: "irrational exuberance" was Alan Greenspan's term for the relationship between the way companies were valued and the way investors felt about their stocks. According to Greenspan, investors used their positive feeling about the market as basis for further investment, investing, in effect, in their own emotions. This phenomenon drove up prices, leading to further exuberance, all of which tended toward the creation of a "bubble"—a term whose own implicit narrative, itself a projection of the stock-market graph, constitutes an answer to any interpretative questions the graph might be said to pose. For Greenspan, the irrationality of irrational exuberance lies in the absence of a connection between feeling and value: irrational exuberance is feeling based "merely" on feeling.[1]

But the circularity that made Greenspan nervous (and along with him, eventually, everyone else)—the idea that the market affects feeling, and feeling affects the market—merely reconfigures a discomfort that has existed at least since Trollope's time: an uneasiness about the unpredictability of investing in shares and the attenuated, indeed, imaginary relationship that obtains between investors and the objects of their investment. Because investors necessarily operate at a distance from the companies or commodities in which they invest, possessing limited if any knowledge of them, they necessarily invest in something other than facts: they invest in narratives about companies and commodities, for instance, and in their own hopes and wishes about those narratives. The term "irrational exuberance," referring both to the market and to the feelings of those who invest in it, seeks to ward off the danger of too much happiness by gesturing toward its unlikely-sounding opposite, rational feeling: the idea that feeling could be an accurate gauge of value. But the attempt to separate rational from irrational feeling is only one of numerous attempts made during the course of stock-exchange history to locate stability in an arena whose essence it is to provide none. From Trollope to Greenspan, discussions about investment and the market have repeatedly sought to draw similar lines: between the solid and the ephemeral, safety and risk—between, in general, value securely located in companies or commodities and value that is only imagined to be there—as a means of countering the uncertainty and unpredictability, indeed, the sheer uninterpretability, of the fluctuating value of shares. Could such lines be fixed, there would be no need for the uncertainties, and the movements of the heart with which we register them, that tie our identities to the market.

Romance and Finance

The CNBC commercial assimilates the movement of stock prices to the biological and metaphorical pulse, condensing in a single image—a videographic palimpsest—a connection that financial narratives from the Victorian period to the present have spelled out, and in doing so reinforced: that between money and the heart. Trollope's *The Prime Minister* might be said to present an uncontroversial understanding of the way this connection works: one can read a man's character, the novel has it, in the way he manages his money. But *The Prime Minister* also offers other ways of understanding our own assimilations of feeling and the market, and the lines we continue to draw in their name, perhaps most strikingly in its status as a precursor of today's stock-market dramas: those episodes, played out in the daily newspapers and the nightly news, in which a violation of financial rules (or merely a suspected one, since such cases do not always involve legal wrongdoing) registers as a general social violation, an offense against middle-class culture and feeling.[2] In offering up as villains stock-market characters whose particular forms of exuberance are routinely characterized as reverberating beyond the market, contemporary culture demonstrates the persistence and the usefulness of a Victorian master narrative that fashions characterological differences around stock-market distinctions.

The established, traditional families in Trollope's *The Prime Minister*, the Whartons and the Fletchers, rely on their feeling as a means of gauging value, but the appearance of a new man—a man of the stock exchange—disrupts their ability to do so. Of the Whartons and the Fletchers, Trollope writes: "As a class they are more impregnable, more closely guarded by their feelings and prejudices against strangers than any other. None keep their daughters to themselves with greater care, or are less willing to see their rules of life changed or abolished. And yet this man, half foreigner half Jew,—and as it now appeared, whole pauper,—had stepped in and carried off a prize for which such a one as Arthur Fletcher was contending!" (662).[3] It is precisely in relation to the feelings and prejudices of this class that the character Ferdinand Lopez poses a problem: about Lopez, throughout much of the first half of *The Prime Minister,* no one knows—though many suspect—what the appropriate feeling might be. Thus when trying to convince his daughter Emily, who has declared herself in love with Lopez, that the man is no gentleman, all Wharton can say with certainty is that "no one knows anything about him, or where to inquire even" (46). And while that ignorance, we are told, would be enough for Dr. Johnson, according to whom "any other derivation for the term 'gentleman' . . . than that which causes it to signify 'a man of ancestry' is whimsical" (10), what troubles Wharton's ability to make his case with conviction is the fact that, as the novel puts it, the nineteenth century admits exceptions. And Ferdinand Lopez is an exception: on the basis of his bearing, his clothing, his man- ner of sitting on a horse, and "the lower half of his face" (12), "It was admitted on all sides that Ferdinand Lopez was a gentleman" (10).[4]

The admission of Ferdinand Lopez as a gentleman constitutes an admission of the impossibility of keeping him out: like the markets, which cannot afford to invest only at home, English society is necessar- ily vulnerable to foreign charm.[5] What allows for Lopez's admission is this:

> We all know the man,—a little man, generally, who moves seldom and softly,—who looks always as if he had just been sent home in a band- box. Ferdinand Lopez was not a little man, and moved freely enough; but never, at any moment,—going into the city or coming out of it, on horseback or on foot, at home over his book or after the mazes of the dance,—was he dressed otherwise than with perfect care. Money and time did it, but folks thought that it grew with him, as did his hair and nails. And he always rode a horse which charmed good judges of what a park nag should be;—not a prancing, restless, giggling, sideway-going, useless garran, but an animal well made, well bitted, and with perfect paces, on whom a rider if it pleased him could be as quiet as a statue on a monument. (13)

It is of course known by Wharton and others that not knowing anything about Lopez is the same as knowing something about him, and that the suspicions hovering around him are likely to resolve into knowledge of a specific kind. Indeed, we are told that his father is Portuguese, and we are invited to suspect that he is a Jew.[6] The novel's gentlemen intuit, as it is the business of gentlemen to do, Lopez's lack of gentlemanly status; "what a gentleman knows" (30) above all is how to identify another gentleman. But in this case, what a gentleman knows can have no practical effect on what Ferdinand Lopez does, for his admission as a gentleman is an admission that nothing can be done about him. The allowance of exceptions to the rule means that gentlemanliness must be determined in each individual case; once exceptions are admitted, each candidate becomes, in effect, a stock, his value in need of assessment. And once the doors to Wharton/Fletcher society, along with questions of gentlemanly identity, are thrown open, the identities of the Whartons and Fletchers—formerly held in place by their strong feelings and prejudices—are also in play.

If the nineteenth century admits exceptions, there is nothing to keep the Ferdinand Lopezes of the world from attending one's social gatherings, meeting one's family, running for Parliament, and marrying one's daughter. Victorian novels typically rely on narratives of romantic love to adjudicate the relationship between feeling and value, the love relationship absorbing and disseminating the codes of ideological discourses such as those of race, nationality and class. It makes sense, then, that the crisis signaled by Lopez's admission into the world of the Whartons and Fletchers should take shape as the novel's romantic plot. But the relation between romance and finance in *The Prime Minister* is more complex than the model of ideological mystification allows, since for Trollope and his readers, as for twentieth- and twenty-first-century subjects of market economies and the narratives that circulate within them, the stock exchange has provided a compellingly coherent set of terms within which familiar cultural narratives, and indeed familiar cultural identities, have been rewritten and reconceived. In the cultural narrative of the stock exchange whose terms are *The Prime Minister*'s, Emily's feeling for Lopez may be understood as the characteristic attitude of the speculator: she must therefore be taught to invest her emotions, as she would her money, wisely. The terms of romance and those of finance are interchangeable, universalized by gender difference: if feeling is a woman's capital (and its signifier, since she also brings her father's wealth to the table), then speculating with love is understandable in relation to, or as an analogy for, speculating with money. Feeling, that is, is a form of currency, and feelings about money are a template for feelings in general: the truth about a character, Trollope contends, may be learned from the way that character feels about money. Thus *The Prime Minister*'s calibration of feeling and value has as much to do with Lopez's financial dealings as it does with his romantic ones; indeed, the former serve as the lens by means of which the true character of the latter will be revealed. But the marriage plot is not exactly, or not only, an analogue for the financial plot, nor is the financial plot simply a framework or metaphor for the domestic one. Rather, the marriage plot *is* the financial plot: the lesson Emily Wharton learns about Lopez is taught by way of her increasing knowledge of his financial dealings. His value—more precisely, his lack of value—emerges for her, as it does in the novel as a whole, in a series of demonstrations of what kind of character he is, speculator or investor—and how his status as one or the other determines Emily's status as well.

Coffee and Guano

After his failed run for Parliament, Lopez accepts payment for his electioneering expenses twice—once from the Duke of Omnium and once from Wharton—without telling the second that he has already been paid by the first. He rationalizes the keeping of both sums:

It was not at the breakfast table that Ferdinand Lopez made up his mind to pocket the Duke's money and to say nothing about it to Mr. Wharton. He had been careful to conceal the cheque, but he had done so with the feeling that the matter was one to be considered in his own mind before he took any step. As he left the house, already considering it, he was inclined to think that the money must be surrendered. Mr. Wharton had very generously paid his electioneering expenses, but had not done so simply with the view of making him a present of the money. He wished the Duke had not taken him at his word. In handing this cheque over to Mr. Wharton he would be forced to tell the story of his letter to the Duke, and he was sure that Mr. Wharton would not approve of his having written such a letter. How could anyone approve of his having applied for a sum of money which had already been paid to him? How could such a one as Mr. Wharton—an old-fashioned English gentleman—approve of such an application being made under any circumstances? Mr. Wharton would very probably insist on having the cheque sent back to the Duke—which would be a sorry end to the triumph as at present achieved. And the more he thought of it the more sure he was that it would be imprudent to mention to Mr. Wharton his application to the Duke. The old men of the present day were, he said to himself, such fools that they understood nothing. And then the money was very convenient to him. . . . By the time, therefore, that he had reached the city he had resolved that at any rate for the present he would say nothing about it to Mr. Wharton. Was it not spoil got from the enemy by his own courage and cleverness? When he was writing his acknowledgment for the money to Warburton he had taught himself to look upon the sum extracted from the Duke as a matter quite distinct from the payment made to him by his father-in-law. (376–77)

In a process that enacts the business it describes—"the more he thought of it the more sure he was"—Lopez provides himself with a rationale for keeping both sums. Gentlemanly behavior matters, to his way of thinking, only to others; it is a performance ("How could anyone approve?") relevant only insofar as it supports or interferes with his plans. And as he teaches himself to look upon two identical payments as distinct, differentiating himself in the process from "the old men of the present day," he displays a characteristic the novel defines elsewhere as an inability to perceive appropriate distinctions: he is a man who "wouldn't mind if he ate horseflesh or beef if horseflesh were as good as beef" (141), and who, most generally, has no feeling for "the lines which separated right from wrong" (373). The movement of his thought—choreographed by the movement of his feet and bounded by his trip from home to city—displays, indeed, not an observance of that line but rather a mental fluidity, an ability to justify the merits of the position he wishes to take.

Not possessing the sensibilities held by the old men of the present day—not knowing what it is that a gentleman knows, but aspiring nevertheless to gentlemanliness—Ferdinand Lopez is necessarily in the position of teaching himself, and others, new ways to look upon things. When his partner, Sexty Parker, expresses concern that "the coffee and guano [in which Lopez has invested] were not always real coffee and guano," Lopez teaches him, daily after lunch, to see things in a different way.

"If I buy a ton of coffee and keep it six weeks, why do I buy it and keep it, and why does the seller sell it instead of keeping it? The seller sells it because he thinks he can do best by parting with it now at a certain price. I buy it because I think I can make money by keeping it. It is just the same as though we were to back our opinions. He backs the fall. I back the rise. You needn't have coffee and you needn't have guano to do this. Indeed the possession of the coffee and the possession of the guano is only a very clumsy addition to the trouble of your profession. . . . " Coffee and guano still had to be bought because the

world was dull and would not learn the tricks of trade as taught by
Ferdinand Lopez . . . but our enterprising hero looked for a time in
which no such dull burden should be imposed upon him. (377)

The world has, of course, since learned the tricks of trade as taught by
Ferdinand Lopez. For Trollope, however, Lopez's failure to distinguish
between the guano that is not there and the guano that is further displays his status as a man who fails to make appropriate distinctions.[7]
Repeatedly documenting Lopez's feelings about money, the novel illustrates in increasingly vivid detail the contention it finally makes explicit:
"He knew how to speak, and how to look, how to use a knife and fork,
how to dress himself, and how to walk. But he had not the faintest
notion of the feelings of a gentleman" (497).

"Teaching to look upon," an activity that Trollope seems here to
disparage, is thus also one whose necessity he admits—for despite the
novel's insistence on the intuitive quality of gentlemanly knowledge,
Abel Wharton no less than Trollope himself had to make his way to it.
And Trollope's awareness of the necessity of such activity leads not to
anarchy, or to *avant-la-lettre* deconstruction, or even to an excessively
threatened social fabric, but rather and in several ways to the novel:
that vehicle *par excellence* both for teaching the nineteenth century how
to look upon things and, in Trollope's case as in others', for securing
the admission of middle-class authors into gentlemanly circles.[8] Indeed,
that Lopez's ambition is also his author's suggests the importance of the
lines this novel attempts to draw. For if the speculator and the novelist
are both seeking to rise in the world by telling stories—stories Trollope
referred to in his own case as his "castles in the air" (*Autobiography*
42)—then a certain strain accompanies the assertion that the true gentleman can be separated from the pretender by means of gentlemanly
intuition.

In an atmosphere in which money seems to have appropriated the
power to create gentlemen, Trollope makes it the business of his novels
to delineate the distinctions in feeling that separate the gentleman from
the non-gentleman: to refine and elaborate the code for an age in which
that elaboration is, he believes, sorely needed. Revealing the contents
of Lopez's mind in order to illustrate distinctions between gentlemanly
values and their absence, Trollope both dramatizes the need his novels
are designed to fulfill and seeks to affirm his own possession of the discourse, his solid grasp of the nature and texture of gentlemanly ideals.
But his contribution to a history of the emotions lies, beyond this, in
his ability to bring money into the realm of feeling, and more signifi-

cantly, to demonstrate that it is already there. For the feelings within which Trollope discerns distinctions are feelings about money: money is the proving ground within which distinctions in feeling appear. In the context of wealth made rapidly and often mysteriously though the buying and selling of shares (a context in which respectability might be built on a foundation of guano, or, even worse, its absence), and in which discourses about money sought to maintain the possibility that respectability and the stock exchange could coexist by marking boundaries between legitimate and illegitimate ways of reaping investment's rewards, the distinction between what was regarded approvingly as investment and what was reviled as speculation turns out, not surprisingly, to be a distinction in feeling as well.[9]

Trollope's emphasis on the role gentlemanly feeling plays in financial matters informs his description of the way Wharton and Lopez came by their money. Wharton, we are told, "had begun his practice early, and had worked in a stuff gown till he was nearly sixty. At that time he had amassed a large fortune, mainly from his profession, but partly also by the careful use of his own small patrimony and by his wife's money. Men knew that he was rich, but no one knew the extent of his wealth" (*PM* 25–26). Here is the corresponding account of Lopez: "He had been on the Stock Exchange, and still in some manner, not clearly understood by his friends, did business in the City. . . . But nobody, not even his own bankers or his own lawyer,—not even the old woman who looked after his linen,—ever knew the state of his affairs" (11). The difference between Wharton's gentlemanliness and Lopez's is, in keeping with Johnson's dictum, a difference in what is known of their ancestry, and the implication is that what this particular lack of knowledge signifies for Lopez's "use" of money is an absence of care. And the line between care and the absence of care is, in general terms, from the nineteenth century to the twenty-first, the line that separates the investor from the speculator.

If the stock-market graph is generally aligned with the movement of feeling, then a close attention to fluctuations of value suggests an identification with impulse itself. Thus while the investor is typically imagined as detached from his money, able to ignore its day-to-day movements, the speculator is viewed as a creature of unregulated impulse and unruly emotion, in thrall, day and night, to his greed. The investor, able to wait for his "emotional payoff" (Schott, 25) is promised in the end an even greater reward, while the speculator serves as a useful embodiment of Victorian bad habits: mental depravity, idleness, deceitfulness.[10]

But the image of the investor waiting patiently for his payoff should alert us to a certain inconsistency in conventional representations of the difference between speculators and investors—a difference that has long rested upon the premise that, when it comes to the business of making money from money, there is a right way and a wrong one. Writes a commentator in 1998, "Wealth accrues from generally right behavior, not from trying to extract the maximum profit out of any situation" (Schott 24). "Generally right behavior," according to this formulation, refers not exactly to not trying to make money, but, as in Carlyle's formula for attaining happiness, to making money without appearing to try to make money—to making money, in effect, while looking carefully in another direction. "Speculation" routinely describes an energetic attention to fluctuations in value, as contrasted with the investor's long-term involvement with "safe" stocks; identified as the placing of money in the service of risky projects, it is associated with terms like "optimism," "hope," and "bubble." But if one seeks to define the term with any precision, and in particular to clarify the distinction between investment and speculation, one discovers not that distinctions cannot be made—on the contrary, everyone can make them—but rather that, in the context of Britain's economy in the nineteenth century no less than our contemporary one, there is hardly an investment that is not, according to the usual definitions, a speculation: "[t]he practice of buying articles of merchandise, or any purchasable commodity whatever, in expectation of a rise of price and of selling the same at considerable advance" (Maunder, qtd. in Mottram 4).

Distinctions between investment and speculation tend to be made on the basis of personal involvement: the investor is said to be emotionally as well as financially committed to the company or commodity to which he lends his money. But both activities posit an attenuated relationship to the substance or commodity being traded; neither investor nor speculator need ever see the coffee or the guano. Differences thus tend to be articulated as matters of degree, assessing the quantity and quality of such intangibles as duration (how long an investor plans to hold a stock before selling) and intent (is the investor primarily interested in building a railroad, or in making money from an expected rise in railway shares?). Moreover, the characteristic charge made against speculators—that their greed involves them in risky enterprises—is also a matter of degree, since the anxieties about risk and instability attached to the term "speculator" are simply amplifications or exaggerations of feelings that attend the buying and selling of shares in general. In the hair-splitting nature of these distinctions, and in particular the failure of academic discourse to arrive at any consensus on the meaning of the terms, it is possible to see that the two categories are characteristically distinguished from one another not by any precise definition of the activities themselves, where difference to this day remains at the level of name-calling (the annals of respectable financial activity include venture capitalists, investment bankers, stockbrokers—anything but speculators), but rather according to particular constellations of feelings and attitudes. The character called the speculator, whose qualities were rapidly assimilated to the villains of nineteenth-century fiction at the same time that investment (or speculation) became the province of middle-class novel readers, served for the Victorians, as he does for us, as a bogeyman whose function it is to make speculation safe for everyone else: to assume for the national psyche the risks of involvement in the market. The term "speculator" marks the line between right and wrong that cannot be perceived in the wavering pattern of the stock-market graph; in particular, it insists on a distinction between respectable and illicit behavior in relation to the always dubious-seeming business of making money from fluctuations in value.[11] The opposition between investment and speculation is meant to secure the possibility that the system of values that defines gentlemanly behavior can coincide with and be revealed through an individual's feelings about money.

Describing the source of Wharton's and Lopez's money, Trollope provides no specific account of the care Wharton has taken. But care is evident in the novel's quiet mystification of Wharton's financial activity, since for neither man is the source of his money revealed. And though we are told repeatedly that Wharton keeps his financial status and that of his children secret, to their detriment, these details are hidden from readers as well. Given the attention the novel devotes to each man's thinking when it comes to Emily, to one another's faults, and to Lopez's financial dealings, its silence about Wharton's finances may be said to echo Wharton's own: to participate in the mystification of money and power whose function it is to secure the line between right behavior and wrong. Trollope's nondivulgence of details here—the silence of a novelist whose signature, we are often reminded, is the precise specification of his characters' income and capital—underscores the point that the distinction between investors and speculators is located less in what they do than in how they are said to feel, and in how we are taught to feel about them.

That Emily Wharton's feeling for Lopez resembles a speculator's projections for his shares—that her feeling about him is irrationally exuberant—we, like her father, suspect but can do nothing about; such truths, like all speculations, can only be perceived retrospectively, once the bubble has burst. While her initial feelings about him are supremely confident—"I do love him, and I shall never love anyone else in the same way" (46)—she must be taught to see that her feelings are as ungrounded as Lopez's own happiness upon receiving large sums of money. Indeed, for Emily, Lopez comes to personify the rapid fluctuations to which, living in the atmosphere of her father's apparently illimitable wealth, she has never before been privy: he proves to be the embodiment of fluctuating value, the man with a stock-ticker for a heart. After receiving a requested loan of £3000 from his father-in-law, for instance, Lopez is elated: "He was overjoyed—so much so that for a while he lost that restraint over himself which was habitual to him. He ate his breakfast in a state of exultation" (224).[12] And yet "almost immediately" he finds himself needing money again. Here is Emily's response: "She endeavoured to judge him kindly, but a feeling of insecurity in reference to his affairs struck her at once and made her heart cold. . . . Surely a large sum to have vanished in so short a time! Something of the uncertainty of business she could understand, but a business must be perilously uncertain if subject to such vicissitudes as these!" (301). The pattern of feeling she begins to observe in her husband and in her married life—a pattern that causes her heart to grow cold, revealing it to be no less a ticker than her husband's—is that of the fluctuating value of shares, the pace of whose movement she cannot, though she tries, assimilate to the "better or worse" of her marriage vows.[13] It is a pattern whose appropriate periodicity she has internalized in her father's house, along with the intuition that she need not—indeed, ought not—know the source of the money that supports her.

Lopez, we learn, is possessed of the power of compelling belief; to this is ascribed Emily's mistaken conviction "that she had found the good man in finding Ferdinand Lopez" (42). His financial success depends, as we see in his relationship with Sexty Parker, on perpetuating his beliefs: on selling himself. Thus his first order of business upon marrying Emily is to teach her to look as he does upon money: "She must be instructed in his ways. She must learn to look upon the world with his eyes. She must be taught the great importance of money." And, more seriously, "He had learned that she had much influence with her father, and she must be taught to use this influence on her husband's behalf" (214). But she resists—indeed, recoils from—his teaching, which requires her to be the conduit of her father's wealth: "He demanded of her the writing of the letter almost immediately. . . . It seemed as though she were seizing the advantage of the first moment of her freedom to take a violent liberty with her father" (220).

That asking her father for money should resemble the "taking" of "a violent liberty" points toward the Oedipal nature of this scenario; in Emily's narrative the symbolic system that identifies money with guano adds to its list sexuality, marking the categories from which respectability requires the keeping of a careful distance.[14] For Emily, knowing the source of her husband's money, and in particular having her father be that source, both demystifies and endangers the hygienic attitude toward money the Wharton/Fletcher class wishes to preserve. The atmosphere of wealth in which Whartons and Fletchers dwell—in which wealth *is* atmosphere, as in the "pretty things" with which Emily surrounds herself after her marriage—is transformed (liquidated) by Lopez into money: "she was told that her household gods had a price put upon them, and that they were to be sold" (337). What Wharton keeps secret from his children is not, of course, that he is wealthy, but rather by how much: it is not the fact of wealth but the details, the numbers, that embody the mystery of parental power, representing that aspect of parental life a child ought not approach too closely. Thus Emily's growing sense of degradation involves not just her husband's financial failure, but the fact that she cannot choose not to know about it; the book of life, once opened (and of course one may say this of Trollope as well) turns out to be the financial page. "Without a moment's hesitation he could catch at the idea of throwing upon her father the burden of maintaining both her and himself! She understood the meaning of this. She could read his mind so far. She endeavoured not to read the book too closely,—but there it was, opened to her wider day by day, and she knew that the lessons which it taught were vulgar and damnable" (338).

The irrationality of Emily's earlier exuberance is both confirmed and balanced by the otherwise inexplicable rush of degradation and self-loathing she experiences after Lopez's suicide: by her own account she is "the woman that he had thrust so far into the mire that she can never again be clean" (643). Her repulsion—and Lopez's Jewishness of course comes into play here—viscerally reinforces the difference between speculator and investor, and the feelings about money embodied in each term take shape as paradigmatically different forms of masculinity, different men, and a lesson about manhood: "[T]here would come upon her unbidden, unwelcome reminiscences of Arthur Fletcher. . . . She remembered his light, wavy hair, which she had loved as one loves the beauty of a dog, which had seemed to her young imagination, to her in the ignorance of her early years to lack something of a dreamed-of manliness. . . . But now,—now that it was all too late,—the veil had fallen from her eyes." And once feelings about money take shape in this way—are embodied as two men—they can be "seen" with absolute clarity: "She could see the difference between manliness and deportment" (338). Indeed, money appears to make everything clear, as Lopez's increasingly bad luck with it seems naturally to accompany and support the revelation that he is a thoroughly bad character. Thus the stock-market narrative substantiates, in an altogether unsurprising way, the differences between Lopez's character and Fletcher's. And it also enables the drawing of another necessary distinction: that between one's father and the "good man" who will be one's husband. In Emily's desire not to know, as in her feeling of repulsion toward her husband and herself, the narrative of speculation, with its moral baggage about greed and the defiling touch of money—and of the Jew—is intertwined with a necessary cultural narrative whose trajectory, with the unmistakable clarity of a plunging line on the stock-market graph, demonstrates the irrationality of her investment in Ferdinand Lopez.

Speculator and Jew

Wharton's failure to stop his daughter's marriage has been ascribed both to a failure of his prejudice—he is not quite prejudiced enough—and to its success: so concerned is he about Lopez's "foreignness" that he fails adequately to scrutinize the man's character. But like other characters in the novel, including his daughter and Lopez, Wharton in fact blunders because he is overidentified with his investment: his ability to evaluate Lopez is clouded by his feeling for his daughter. Indeed, as he considers Emily's feeling for Lopez he is unable to maintain the distinction of which he had previously been so certain.

> But then was he sure that he was right? He of course had his own way of looking at life, but was it reasonable that he should force the girl to look at things with his eyes? The man was distasteful to him as being unlike his idea of an English gentleman, and as being without those far-reaching fibres and roots by which he thought that the stability and solidity of a human tree should be assured. But the world was changing about him every day. Royalty was marrying out of its degree. Peers' sons were looking only for money. And, more than that, peers' daughters were bestowing themselves on Jews and shopkeepers. Had he not better make the usual inquiry about the man's means, and, if

satisfied on that head, let the girl do as she would? Added to all this, there was growing on him a feeling that ultimately youth would as usual triumph over age, and that he would be beaten. If that were so, why worry himself, or why worry her? (75)

Wharton's thoughts display not the unwavering certainty of the clear moral line but rather the jittery peaks and valleys of the stock-market graph; his willingness to entertain the possibility of Ferdinand Lopez as a son-in-law—to overlook a distinction he had previously considered crucial—takes shape as a mental wavering, one not wholly dissimilar from that manifested by Lopez as he teaches himself to distinguish between two identical payments. Tracing the fluctuating movement of characters' thoughts as they wend their way from one side of a question to the other, Trollope gives narrative form and identity to those peaks and valleys. But the identity such thoughts suggest, as they cross and recross the lines that separate right from wrong, is one not organized enough to take a stand on one side or the other: it is identity that, finding no solid ground but its own conclusions, is in the position of backing itself, of founding feeling on feeling. Indeed, the pattern of Wharton's thoughts here mimics the uncertain status of Ferdinand Lopez himself, whose admission into polite society threatens its solid values: not because that society doesn't "know," as a gentleman knows, what kind of a man he is, but rather because it cannot locate the line he has crossed, nor can it draw one that will keep him out. It is up to the novel, then—and not only Trollope's, but the whole gamut of evil-speculator novels of the period—to do what novels do best, which is to draw that line: to harden suspicion into narrative, to fix the trajectory of Lopez's life into a recognizable pattern, to vivify distinctions in feeling by embodying them in characters.

The beginning of *The Prime Minister* keeps the status of Lopez's Jewishness mysterious: it invites us to wonder whether he is, in fact, a Jew. Suspicion, as in those "disagreeable matters" Lopez hopes will not come up for discussion, creates a distinction waiting to be made, an outline that requires filling in. But suspecting Lopez of being a Jew is not, of course, reason enough to convict him. Nor, it turns out, is his status as speculator; indeed, the need to produce for Lopez a spate of "other" bad qualities, including the careless treatment of his wife, his deceitfulness, and his commission of the actual crime of forgery invites not so much the conclusion that speculators are evil as the suspicion that perhaps they are not quite evil enough. The series of mishaps that leads Lopez to suicide suggests on the part of the novelist what market analysts call "magical thinking"—something is so because I have wished it to be—distinguishable only from the novelist's usual business, if at all, by the palpability of its need. Making Lopez a Jew and a criminal is the equivalent of wanting the guano to be real, the equivalent of narratives that "explain" what the market is doing: it is a stock-market story, an attempt to secure feelings and beliefs in something outside the self.[15]

Just as Lopez's Jewishness functions simultaneously as a figure for the unknown (no one knows his background) and as an image of absolute predictability (reinforcing the suspicion that he will, and deserves to, come to a bad end), so too does the end of the novel substantiate the suspicions it has aroused about him and, at the same time, devote itself to flogging all the reality out of his identity. Having lost everything in speculation, he throws himself under a train and is "knocked into bloody atoms" (520). But his clothes reveal no signs of identity: he carries no papers, and his handkerchief and collar bear no mark. "The fragments of his body set identity at defiance, and even his watch had been crumpled into ashes" (524). Hammering his point home, as another nail in the coffin, Trollope has it discovered five months later that Lopez has signed Sexty Parker's name to a bill, effectively ruining Parker's wife and children. "He had been all a lie from head to foot" (606). But Lopez is not exactly a lie: like the stories periodically found to circulate in the market—stories designed to affect its movement despite their failure to reflect the status of actual stocks or commodities; stories whose authors must be discovered, punished, and never allowed to trade again—his is not so much a false story as it is a shadow story, a trope for the market itself, which at such moments reveals the depth of its investment in storytelling, constituting itself as a necessary clearing-house for the separation of true narratives from false ones. And it is a trope for Trollope as well, as he tells us the story of a man who looks, dresses, and sits on a horse like a gentleman but is not one. And we know he is not because, we are told, the stories he tells are not the right kind of stories.[16]

Veering between exuberance and self-loathing, Emily Wharton defines the boundaries between which, Trollope suggests, feelings about money characteristically waver; that her emotions appear spontaneous and visceral, and are mediated through men, naturalizes emotions whose financial bearing the novel elaborates more directly elsewhere. Intertwining personal drama and financial crisis, Emily's story incorporates money into the familial narrative: just as she recoils from herself in horror, as from the contents of her husband's mind, so too may the state of one's money seem to echo—or does it produce?—the state of one's emotions. Such narratives facilitate the transfer of identity into numbers that is capitalism's lifeblood; in the elation or self-loathing that attends the fluctuation of the numbers we pursue our own self-regulation, an ideal self embodied in the fantasy of an ideal number. Exploring the painful consciousness that signifies a failure to keep one's proper distance from money, however, Emily's narrative in fact suggests how attending to the numbers may help us avoid such a consciousness, structuring our proper relation to money and the market. For the numbers, possessing the lure of authenticity and simultaneously refusing to give anything away—to reveal what the "real" story is—offer us the feeling that we know even as they tell us nothing: even as they serve as substitutes for whatever it is they might tell. Thus while keeping us focused on the drama of their movement—on the roller-coaster ride that constitutes the narrative of the market's ups and downs—they allow us to keep our feet, or so it seems, out of the guano. After the narrative of Lopez's exuberance, of Emily's mistake, and of the degradation that results from their entanglement comes the embrace of what might now have to be called rational exuberance: the ordinary happiness of the married, middle-class subject, whose choice, shaped by life's hard lessons, is articulated by that narrative as a choice of investment over speculation. One might choose otherwise; in some cases, one has done so, and may do so again. To know this is to acknowledge the compelling quality of the line we have learned to straddle, and of the numbers we continue to look upon for what they seem to tell us about ourselves.[17]

CHAPTER FOUR

David Copperfield's Happiness Economics

Ask yourself whether you are happy, and you cease to be so.
To know that a feeling would make me happy if I had it,
did not give me the feeling. . . .
—John Stuart Mill, Autobiography

O, we were happy, we were happy!
—Charles Dickens, David Copperfield

David Copperfield's narrative is punctuated by moments of which David remarks, as he does of an evening once passed with his mother and his nurse Peggotty, "we were very happy." Including a chapter entitled "One Happy Afternoon," sprinkled throughout with references to "my happier childhood" and "the happy old home," Dickens's novel registers these moments as emotional touchstones: reading the Crocodile Book with Peggotty; walking on the sand at Yarmouth with Little Em'ly; attended bedside by his mother, in a pre-Murdstonian moment of bliss.[1] Rather than attend to the specificity of each of these scenes, however, I want to explore the text's, and David's own, assimilation of them to a single term and a single emotional trajectory.

Were it simply the case that Dickens wished for his hero a happy ending, the novel would differ little in this sense from many others. But *David Copperfield*'s drumbeat repetition of the term "happy" sets it apart, recalling another well-known Victorian text with a similar emphasis: that section of John Stuart Mill's *Autobiography* in which Mill asks himself whether, were he to achieve all the goals he has set for himself, he would be happy. In both cases, the insistent use of the term "happiness" invites, even as it seems to foreclose, consideration of what the word might be said to mean; in both cases, what looks like a simultaneous attachment to the term and detachment from the self supposed to feel it raises the question of why one would ask oneself whether one is happy, or think it necessary to announce—to oneself or to others—that one is. The attachment of the self to the word happiness, along with the tracking of that feeling's arrival and departure (as Micawber tracks and aligns his quantities of happiness and money) recalls *The Prime Minister*'s alignment of emotions and shares, with "happiness" standing as the element to be tracked: that which seems to render possible an accurate—because distant—reading of the self.[2]

An Average Happiness

Toward the end of Dickens's novel, after the departure of her shadowy double, Martha, Little Em'ly despairs of her inability to have the feeling she knows would make her happy.

> Oh, pray, aunt, try to help me! Ham, dear, try to help me! Mr. David, for the sake of old times, do, please, try to help me! I want to be a better girl than I am. I want to feel a hundred times more thankful than I do. I want to feel more, what a blessed thing it is to be the wife of a good man, and to lead a peaceful life. Oh me, oh me! Oh, my heart, my heart! (349)

With an aggressiveness that belies contemporary criticism's usual understanding of ideology's ability to influence the subject undetected—to penetrate a subject's defenses unknown and unperceived, like an X-ray—this passage registers the weight of the compulsion, characteristic of our own culture no less than the Victorians', to name happiness the thing that one feels. Indeed, the insistence on the word in Mill's account of his paralyzing depression and in Dickens's novel points toward the problem of knowledge Em'ly's words, like Mill's, intimate: that happiness seems most secure, most knowable, when eyed from a distance—as something to orient oneself toward rather than something with which one can coincide. This may be the case not because happiness, in accordance with some universal rule, is unattainable, nor because only some are good enough to attain it—though as Em'ly's example suggests, Victorian domestic ideology goes to some lengths to assert the latter. Rather, the word "happiness" as used in the texts and cultural discourses discussed here implies the comparison of the self to a set of culturally determined requirements. Frequently the subject of a question posed by others ("are you happy?"), the term may just as easily be (and is, necessarily, at the same time, as Mill finds), the subject of a question posed to oneself—the desire to name one's feeling "happiness," often haunted, it seems, by the very absence of spontaneity and natural feeling the word is supposed to imply. This chapter shows how the term "happiness" evokes the gap described above in the form of the question it implies, and is invoked at the same time to close it by allowing a clear comparison between the status of one self and another.

Because the texts discussed here point toward and in many ways summarize issues discussed elsewhere in this book—the average man of *Middlemarch;* Lopez's irrational exuberance; Emily Wharton's romantic speculations—I have departed from the novels' own chronology, placing my reading of *David Copperfield* after those of *Middlemarch, Little Dorrit,* and *The Prime Minister.* I depart even further, to begin with, by bringing to bear on Mill's *Autobiography* and Dickens's novel two contemporary, nonliterary accounts whose understanding of happiness as implying narratives of quantification and comparison echo, and may help to explain, the assumptions that structure these Victorian texts.

WHEN ECONOMISTS in the 1980s began to supplement their annual accounting of the goods and money nations produce with measurements of the national happiness, they rendered explicit the phenomena discussed above, in which happiness prompts a question—a question, moreover, that requires respondents to consult what might be called an internalized version of the average man. For, lacking any obvious way to measure happiness, these economists relied (and continue to rely) on surveys, asking people whether they were happy and how happy they were, and attaching numerical scores or monetary values to the results.[3] "You can," writes a twenty-first century expositor of the science of happiness, "answer questions like: how valuable is a 'marriage' in one's life—how does it compare, for example, with a job that pays twice the salary?" Writes another, "The basic idea is to take large nationwide surveys with data on income and marriage status, together with qualitative questions such as 'do you feel you are playing a useful part in things?' or even self-reported assessments of 'levels of happiness'" (Mukerjee).

Quantifying happiness in true Gradgrindian fashion, happiness economists bring the ostensibly personal and irreducible within the realm of accounting and measurement.[4] In doing so they participate in and reinforce the consolidation of feeling and identity I have discussed throughout this book, as in the *mise-en-abyme* that structures *Middlemarch*'s construction of character, in which interiority turns out to be occupied by numerous imaginary others like oneself, or as in the distinction between different kinds of happinesses that accompanies particular economic and romantic affiliations in *The Prime Minister*. They suggest, in fact, a translation via happiness of complex social interactions into a readable trajectory and an assimilation of diverse affects into a collective emotional identity. Thus happiness economics brings out what is already implied in the prevalent use of the term itself: the idea of a simple and unified emotional reality. Seeking to transform into science the activity I have called distant reading, assigning to the term "happiness" a series of quantifiable elements and representations, happiness economics does what many graphs do as well: it assimilates disparate persons and experiences to a simplified, quantifying narrative.

Comparative Happinesses

Writing in 1985, the sociologist Juliet Schor ascribed the apparent absence of a clear correlation between happiness and money (as discovered by the work of happiness economists) to the role of what she calls "reference groups." When people consider how well off they are, she writes, they tend to compare themselves to others, and in recent years have increasingly chosen as objects of comparison figures far removed from themselves in social and economic status: persons or fictional characters whose images and possessions, displayed on television, in film, and on glossy magazine pages reflect neither the viewers' own situations nor any they might realistically hope to attain. Schor's discussion refers to the kind of highly stratified society characterized by what Thorstein Veblen has called "invidious distinctions": a society in which money and happiness are so closely linked to one another—so "hardwired"—that the lesson of their separation must repeatedly be insisted upon. This is a society, Veblen argues, descended from earlier communities in which visible success, as in the ownership of food or goods, was a result of force. "Aggression [was] . . . the accredited form of action, and booty . . . *prima facie* evidence of successful aggression" (10). Neither the replacement of violence by other ways of acquiring wealth nor the changing nature of the prize, Veblen argues, alters the fundamental nature of the struggle: at the root of the desire for ownership remains "emulation," the imitation of that which confers esteem (17).

The term "happy," as in the question "are you happy?" seems to offset the ostensible distinctiveness of "you" with the abstractness of "happy" in the service of an unspoken democratic ideal: the notion that happiness cannot be defined because its meaning will vary for each individual. But both Veblen and Schor, like the happiness economists, point toward the way in which the question also effectively does away with individuality, asking respondents to consult a mental roster of comparisons and locate themselves within it: to fill the vacancy of the term with a recognizable image, a token in some agreed-upon happiness currency. The insistence on the term "happiness" as the name for what is valued, asked about and measured implies both the sameness of what is desired and the equiva-lent desires of those who are asked. Constructed, as happiness economics constructs it, as currency, happiness becomes part of the narrative of more or less that characterizes Veblen's society of invidious distinctions.

As long as one is aware that someone else possesses more money or things than oneself, Schor's argument goes, one will be dissatisfied, and consumer culture thrives on such dissatisfaction. "If we aped the guy in the corner office once and that was the end of it," she writes, "it would be a relatively minor issue. The difficulty is the dynamic aspect of keep-ing up: the emulation process never ends . . . having *more* is hardwired into our psyches. We are not satisfied with whatever level we have" (*Overspent* 98).[5] But the cultural construction of happiness in the texts I discuss here appears not exactly as a concern with keeping up with the Joneses, but as a somewhat more complex configuration in which a search for personal happiness is filtered through, and constructed in relation to, representations of the happinesses of others, including other potential versions of the self—a construction Schor herself suggests when, collapsing the distinction between interiority and exteriority, she writes that a reference group exists most significantly not in material form, but rather as "a mental category, a comparison concept a person carries around in his or her head" (28). If what one has within one's head is a comparison concept, consisting of possible similarities to or shades of difference between oneself and others, then any notion of a single or stable interiority has been replaced by an image of relationship: the self as an effect of a comparison with others.

Happiness as Distant Reading

Jeremy Bentham famously put happiness on a scale, trying to imagine a society capable of offering the greatest happiness to the greatest number of its members.[6] He was followed in this project by John Stuart Mill, who similarly quantified happiness—thought of it as a uniform substance of which people could possess different amounts—but differed in his sense of the happiness or good a society should emphasize. In his more personal writing, however, Mill, like his colleague Thomas Carlyle, expatiated on the difficulties inflicted upon him by what might be called a happiness imperative—the idea that he should be happy—and the discovery, following perhaps inevitably from this imperative, that he was not. The idea that a person should be happy, and that there might be some good, perhaps even ideal quantity of happiness that he or she must possess, constitutes happiness, I have suggested, as a currency: something to inquire about and assess; something to use for the purpose of comparing oneself to others or to some other version of oneself. Thus when John Stuart Mill and David Copperfield take the measure of their happiness, it is not surprising that comparison concepts come into play. Here is Mill:

> From the winter of 1821, when I first read Bentham, and especially from the commencement of the Westminster Review, I had what might truly be called an object in life: to be a reformer of the world. My conception of my own happiness was entirely identified with this object. . . . I was accustomed to felicitate myself on the certainty of a happy life which I enjoyed, through placing my happiness in something durable and distant, in which some progress might always be making, while it could never be exhausted by complete attainment. This did very well for several years. . . . But the time came when I awakened from this as from a dream. It was in the autumn of 1826. I was in a dull state of nerves, such as everybody is occasionally liable to; unsusceptible to enjoyment or pleasurable excitement. . . . In this frame of mind it occurred to me to put the question directly to myself: "Suppose that all your objects in life were realized; that all the changes in institutions and opinions which you are looking forward to, could be completely effected at this very instant: would this be a great joy and happiness to you?" And an irrepressible self-consciousness distinctly answered: "No!" At this my heart sank within me; the whole foundation on which my life was constructed fell down. All my happiness was to have been found in the continual pursuit of this end. The end had ceased to charm, and

how could there ever again be any interest in the means? I seemed to have nothing left to live for. (86–87)

If there is a generally unemphasized element of the miserly in this account—"I was accustomed to felicitate myself on the certainty of a happy life which I enjoyed"—that element may serve here as an indication of the thoroughness, and indeed casualness, with which modern discussions of happiness tend to be structured in economic terms. Mill's description of his pre-crisis self evokes the image of an undisruptable security—an imagining of the future as money in the bank—and suggests, rather than any unconscious and immediate pleasure, the keeping of an eye on his happiness account. His assertion of the correspondence between the end and the means is not, however, confirmed by his report that, as soon as he discovers the solace offered him by music, he grows "tormented by the exhaustability of musical combinations" (94); rather, Mill here seems depressed by the idea that he might ever reach the end of any project, including the reformation of the world.

If the idea of happiness on the investment model initially works for Mill, that is, the idea that this process will come to an end, yielding a return, does not; it is as if Trollope's Abel Wharton had suddenly turned speculator, his notion of the good way of making money suddenly transformed into the bad. The issue may not be, however, as Mill suggests, that "the end had ceased to charm," but rather that the pressure placed on the word "happiness" as a consolidating entity during this period—the work it is called upon to do for the individual—makes it available for, and indeed defines it as a means of accomplishing, what I have been calling distant reading. The pattern of thought used to understand the stock market, that is—the reduction of complexity to a simple trajectory that either rises or falls—is the same pattern of thought evoked by the term happiness, which both mediates between the individual and the social and smooths out any bumps that might appear along the way. "Happiness" as these texts use it looks at the self from the outside, evoking the same desire for (and illusion of) control the investor seeks as he tracks the rise and fall of his stocks. Indeed, the reason that what might appear to be an anachronistic use of twentieth-century sociological theory—Veblen and Shor—works for Dickens and Mill, as I wish to argue it does, is that in the nineteenth century happiness becomes an object of distant reading: not only in the sense suggested by Veblen's notion of conspicuous consumption (the embodiment of happiness in material things, such as a car or a house), but also in the sense that as the focus of ideological concern, designated as that which "everyone" wants, the term offers the respondent a way to evaluate how he is doing as he aligns himself with others on a metaphorical meter or scale.

Asking himself the happiness question, Mill structures his relation to his feelings—or rather, reveals that they are structured (as they continue to be in the cultural cure he decides on as a solution) indirectly, as if approaching himself in this distant way—getting a read on his happiness level—will somehow provide a solution to the problem. In fact, of course, it merely points toward the way a term ideologically attached to the personal, meant to express a profound truth about the self, operates instead as a means of managing feeling—offering, in Mill's case as in David Copperfield's, a standardized image or series of images in relation to which individual experience can be gauged. Thus it makes sense that Mill finds relief in literary representation: in a picture of happiness routed through and affirmed by the imagined happinesses of imagined others.[7]

According to Mill's analysis of his mental crisis, the principles of associationalist psychology taught him by his father, on which he had based his dedication to the project of reforming the world, failed to sustain his pleasure because the attachments this method created were not natural but artificial. Seeking natural attachments and natural feelings, he turns to literature, and after much futile reading finds his emotional numbness cured by a passage in Marmontel.

> I was reading, accidentally, Marmontel's "Memoires," and came to the passage which relates his father's death, the distressed position of the family and the sudden inspiration by which he, a mere boy, felt and made them feel that he would be everything to them—would supply the place of all that they had lost. A vivid conception of the scene and its feelings came over me, and I was moved to tears. From this moment my burthen grew lighter. . . . I gradually found that the ordinary incidents of life could again give me some pleasure; that I could again find enjoyment, not intense, but sufficient for cheerfulness, in sunshine and sky, in books, in conversation, in public affairs; and that there was, once more, excitement, though of a moderate kind, in exerting myself for my opinions, and for the public good. (91)

Readers of the *Autobiography* traditionally note the Oedipal quality of Mill's response to this passage, and indeed it seems clear that he blames his father for his emotional distress.[8] But this passage more importantly describes a moment of emotional triumph: a winning moment, antithetical to the narrative of having one's happiness "entirely identified" with the "durable and distant" project of reforming the world. The boy who makes his family feel he is everything to them, that he can fill "the place of all they had lost," is not the same as the one whose happiness can be found in world-reformation, subordinated to an "all" that must be everything to him. This latter boy is not at the periphery of his world but rather at its center; not absorbed in the mass but rather "everything" to everyone else. And that everyone else is, inextricably from the passage's expression of what will soon be recognized as a quintessentially Victorian reference for the term "happiness," a family. For if happiness is an emotional currency, its tokens must be fungible; if it is to function successfully as an ideological construction, there must be general consent as to what those tokens are. Mill in this passage, and Dickens in *David Copperfield*—indeed, Dickens throughout his work—respond to, and especially in the latter's case crucially help to construct, images of happiness capable of earning "everyone's" willing consent. The term "happiness" mediates the self's relation to the social whole, at the same time mediating an individual's relation to his own experience. These familial images construct a currency of personal happiness references, a market of domestic images in which individual feeling may be invested.[9]

The scene (and of course it is crucial, here as in *David Copperfield*, that it is a scene, for novelistic representation enables distant reading) offers a specifically familial egotistical pleasure, only barely undercut by Mill's compulsive redirection of it toward his father's project. Indeed, Mill's account of his response to this passage—like his asking of the happiness question—might be said to mark a transition from a long-term commitment to (or investment in) a relatively abstract image of world-reformation to an attachment to a more immediately-gratifying image of domesticity: a scene in which he can see himself. The culture of the feelings Mill finds in this passage (and soon after in Wordsworth) makes sympathetic feeling its primary value, but in its cultivation of and appeal to emotional response positions the individual at its center—a center, as Mill's "vivid conception of the scene and its feelings" suggests, itself constituted by a particular image of the group and his membership in it. It is a structure that, in its domestic mode, shapes the representation of happiness on which Mill and others come to rely, and becomes the Victorian answer to the happiness question.[10]

Mill's account of his response to the Marmontel passage positions him in a detached relation to his own emotions, able to know what he feels only when he comes upon what suddenly appears to him, in a structure of recognition reminiscent of Althusser's account of the workings of ideology, as its representation.[11] This scenario of identification suggests a *mise-en-abyme* in which happiness is difficult to imagine outside generalized representations of the happiness of others—or, in the context of happiness economics, without the aid of numbers or graphs that translate into the arena of official, scientifically validated reality the reported experience of the average man. Within the context of such a reading, identity—like happiness—is necessarily a collective construct, a product of distant reading, since only by referring to some agreed-upon notion of happiness can one know or evaluate one's own. Mill in this much-discussed episode and David Copperfield in Dickens's novel share a tendency to situate themselves in relation to such images: to construct happiness as a series of externalized representations whose purpose is to manage, and provide a concrete answer for, some inchoate and unnameable dissatisfaction.

Snugness

David Copperfield's happiness moments point toward an idealized state of present-ness: a condition outside narrative, conflict, and change ("As to any sense of inequality, or youthfulness, or other difficulty in our way, little Em'ly and I had no such trouble, because we had no future. We made no more provision for growing older, than we did for growing younger" [49]; "I write of her just as she was when I had gone to bed after this talk, and she came to bid me good night" [37]). Like the Marmontel scene, these images vivify an abstraction, providing representations or objective correlatives for the term "happiness" that exclude the inchoate and undecipherable. At the same time the novel's reliance on a single term—the referral of details, characters, and what might be imagined as the distinctive affect of each of these moments to its abstract rubric—transmutes the particularity of each experience into a currency of the same: an economics of happiness. These moments are referents, or reference points: a library of happiness images to which David refers. And his reliance on them to evoke and represent his feeling structures happiness in this text as fundamentally vicarious: as an identification with representation.[12]

David's happiness in the novel is often registered in descriptions of his physical surroundings: interior scenes that, like the domestic drama Mill fixes on in Marmontel, or Eliot's articulation of Lydgate's relation to the common in *Middlemarch*, reflect a construction of the self as an effect of his relation to others. Wondering whether he is to be "the hero of his own life, or whether that station will be occupied by some-one else," David is of course positioned from the novel's beginning in vicarious relation to his own character; as critics have long noted, his relation to other characters tends to be vicarious as well. But the term "vicariousness" only begins to describe the multiple levels of reflection that characterize David's relation to other characters and to himself. As he makes his way from one place to another, for instance, each bed-room offered to David serves as an image of how much psychic room those offering it have reserved for him. Following his exile from his own home, for example—after he has been displaced from his central position in mother's house by the arrival of the Murdstones and a baby brother—the Peggotty boathouse appears to him as the most perfect of spaces.

> If it had been Aladdin's palace, roc's egg and all, I suppose I could not
> have been more charmed with the romantic idea of living in it. There
> was a delightful door cut in the side, and it was roofed in, and there
> were little windows in it; but the wonderful charm of it was, that it
> was a real boat which had no doubt been upon the water hundreds
> of times, and which had never been intended to be lived in, on dry
> land. That was the captivation of it to me. If it had ever been meant to
> be lived in, I might have thought it small, or inconvenient, or lonely;
> but never having been designed for any such use, it was the perfect
> abode. (41)

His own on-board quarters are no less pleasing:

> Peggotty opened a little door and showed me my bedroom. It was
> the completest and most desirable bedroom ever seen—in the stern of
> the vessel; with a little window, where the rudder used to go through;
> a little looking-glass, just the right height for me, nailed against the
> wall, and framed with oyster-shells; a little bed, which there was just
> enough room to get into; and a nosegay of seaweed in a blue mug on
> the table. (42)

If the completeness of this vessel is tied to its smallness or snugness (the latter a term of frequent approbation in the novel, suggesting the snugness of a happiness that is all one's own), that quality also reflects the extent to which the bedroom has been imagined so as to have "just enough room" for its inhabitant and, crucially, no room for anyone else. Indeed, an absence of such completeness characterizes places in the novel less reflective of David's happiness: places that, while they may have room for him, reflect the presence of others as well.

Visiting Steerforth at home during a school holiday, for instance, David's complacent satisfaction in the snugness of his room is abruptly terminated when he suddenly glimpses in one corner a picture of Rosa Dartle.

> Steerforth's room was next to mine, and I went in to look at it. It was a picture of comfort, full of easy chairs, cushions, and footstools, worked by his mother's hand, and with no sort of thing omitted that could help to render it complete. Finally, her handsome features looked down on her darling from a portrait on the wall, as if it were even something to her that her likeness should watch him while he slept.
>
> I found the fire burning clear enough in my room by this time, and the curtains drawn before the windows and round the bed, giving it a very snug appearance. I sat down in a great chair upon the hearth to meditate upon my happiness; and had enjoyed the contemplation of it for some time, when I found a likeness of Miss Dartle looking eagerly at me from above the chimney-piece. (306)

The second room, in its relation to the first, recalls one of those television or movie mirrors that reflects someone other than the person looking into it. If Steerforth's room is rendered complete by the supervisory maternal gaze somewhat redundantly installed there, the visitor's, rather than being completed by a mother's gaze, is marred by the image of a figure whose special subject is, in fact, David's incompleteness when compared to Steerforth. Indeed, the portraits in each case echo the structure and function of the rooms, which in turn reflect their occupants, situating the first boy at the center of the maternal universe and the second, already displaced from that position, off-key and off-balance. Moreover, the side-by-side positioning of the two rooms, two boys, and two pictures structures happiness not as spontaneous, immediate, and intuitive, but rather as position-dependent, comparative, and ever-receding. The second—a disruption or deformation, an incomplete copy or frustrated imitation—of the first, not only reflects a situation of which David has not been imagined as the emotional center, but suggests a definition of happiness less as a given (something we instinctively recognize because it springs from within) than as an imitation or copy, an attempt to reproduce in oneself (one's home, one's possessions) something one has been taught to call happiness. The rooms suggest, indeed, a definition of happiness less as something one knows when one feels it than as something one knows because one has seen it: happiness as a product of invidious comparison. To install David in Steerforth's room is to invite him to measure himself against Steerforth; to invite him to see himself, in comparison, as not happy. But as Rosa Dartle's ghostly presence suggests, the happiness this room reflects is not David's, nor is it intended to be one with which his readers will identify.

Money and Happiness

In *The Female Thermometer,* Terry Castle identifies "a new male type" in the mid-eighteenth century: "the man who must abide in the nonheroic realms of bourgeois existence . . . whose internal 'weather,' so to speak, obsessively charted, has become his sole remaining source of interest" (34). The nineteenth-century version of this subject is focused outward as well as inward, those who invest in their culture's dominant representations of happiness properly—at least in promise—repaid for making that investment: emotionally, in images of coherent identity that align the individual with a larger group; materially, in the realization of a vocation or amount of wealth that results from having read the stock market—and hence one's own internal "weather"—correctly. The idea of investing in happiness stabilizes, in the form of a concrete object or goal, a quality more frequently characterized as unlikely to endure from moment to moment.

Thus David Copperfield's happiness moments necessarily exist within the context they seek to transcend: despite their evocation of an eternal present, they are tinged with the knowledge that the David who was, at a certain moment, happy, is an object of reflection for the David who knows where that happiness went, and for readers as well, who either know or suspect where it is going. When David says of his wedding to Dora, for instance, "I never was so happy" (616), readers—and David as well—know that it is only his naiveté speaking, that the story is far from over, and that his happiness in this moment hinges, as Aunt Betsy reminds him when she warns him away from disciplining Dora, on his ability to suspend questions about his feeling's nature or depth. Complete as these moments seem, that is, they are suspended within and contextualized by the narrative that surrounds them, compromised by what comes before and after. Insofar as a happiness moment assumes a fixed condition, that is, it represents a mistake—what might be called a happiness mistake—similar to the one Mill makes when he asks himself whether, were he to achieve his object in life, he would be happy. For the existence of these moments and the effect of the surrounding narrative on them reveal a tension between happiness imagined as a never-changing ideal, on the one hand, and happiness understood as shifting series of representations to which its subjects must respond—an ongoing narrative of more and less, of keeping up with an always-moving image of the self—on the other. In this latter capacity, happiness might be said to resemble money, and David's collection of happiness moments an attempt at accumulation or hoarding. And if the drawing of that analogy (between happiness and money) seems crude or crass—perhaps Gradgrindian—one need only turn for the authority to make it to that celebrated character for whom the connection between money and happiness, and the narrative of instability that brings them together, become vital.

"Annual income twenty pounds, annual expenditure nineteen pounds ought and six, result happiness. Annual income twenty pounds, annual expenditure twenty pounds ought and six, result misery" (186). For Micawber, money is the currency of happiness, as well as a kind of happiness meter: a way of tracking its comings and goings. His account of the relation between money and happiness has the status of what Roland Barthes calls an inoculation: so baldly stated, so laughable, that it cannot possibly be taken as true. But in fact Micawber's instability, his vulnerability to the alternating increase and decrease of his finances, exemplifies the very condition David's happiness moments exist to subvert. For Micawber captures in the form of a caricature (so one need not really believe in it) the status of the middle-class subject in an economy in which the fluctuating status of one's money is likened to the ebb and flow of a vital bodily fluid: a society to which money is so crucial that a confusion between money and happiness—as in the imagined substitution of one indispensable substance for another—might sometimes, understandably (but, we are always reminded, mistakenly) occur. For such a character, the appearance of money (like the sight of one's own blood) heralds its disappearance, in a process that should teach its owner never to rest easy in the place—and certainly not the furniture—it may have purchased. In the economy of Victorian middle-class identity, Micawber's character tells us, an individual's relation to happiness, like his relation to money, must consist of a refusal of complacency (thus the asking of the money question—do I have enough?—is analogous to the asking of the happiness question, and the answer to both is the same): the riding of an emotional wave whose arrival is no less certain than is its subsequent and inevitable disappearance.

If Mrs. Micawber's repeated vow—"I never will desert Mr. Micawber"—serves to balance her husband's volatility, suggesting an unchanging state of assured happiness (happiness as the absence of economics), Micawber's own characterization of the relationship between income and happiness points toward the emotional narrative such assertions would paper over: a registering of tremors and imbalances, the susceptibility of feeling and the identity it crystallizes to the vicissitudes of time and change. But Micawber's formula also suggests the extent to which the abstraction "happiness" summarizes and distances, conceptualizing emotion as currency, as an abstract flow to be tracked. What is significant about Micawber's tag-line, that is, is less its seemingly comical declaration that happiness comes and goes with income than its implicit characterization of happiness as a quantifiable substance whose levels fluctuate in the same way that money does.[13]

David Copperfield seeks not money but happiness. And yet even as he seems to ride the ebb and flow of a happiness unmediated by money, the novel's reliance on his happiness moments as a kind of emotional gold standard implies a metaphorical substitution of one for the other. Like many Victorian novels, *David Copperfield* insists on the subordination of money to happiness. But even as it does so it inscribes happiness within what looks like a monetary system, representing it as an object of desire only few deserve and even fewer can possess. Ostensibly elevating happiness over money, that is, the novel in fact ties its characters to this single abstraction, imposing on them a uniform desire: not representing money as happiness, but rather constituting representations of happiness as its vital currency. And since those who surround David are constructed, as he is, as subjects of happiness, they are necessarily his competitors, their share in the novel's emotional rewards—the extent to which they deserve what he deserves—the focus of scrupulous attention.[14]

For *David Copperfield's* insistent use of the term "happiness" signals not that every character may, in democratic fashion, construe that state according to his or her own desires, but rather that the novel's references for it tend to be everywhere the same. Alongside the novel's detailed accounts of places and rooms, for instance, the intense and ongoing drama of David and Steerforth and the insistently-returned-to distinctions between David and Uriah Heep situate differences between rivals—for affection, status, "place"—at the novel's emotional center. But *David Copperfield* also specializes in the relentless recording of small distinctions, visible to David's alert eye for them and magnified, simply, by the sheer fact of being noticed. This novel's particular version of happiness, that is, enables David to situate every character on a scale in relation to himself, and to evaluate his own position in relation to others. David's good friend Traddles, for instance, not only serves as a foil for David but has, at the time of David's courtship of Dora, a foil courtship of his own, and hence also a bride to serve as a foil for David's and an affection in relation to which David's own can be glorified. Thus David: "I encouraged him to talk about Sophy, on the way; which he did with a loving reliance on her that I very much admired. I compared her *in my mind* with Dora, with considerable inward satisfaction; but I candidly admitted to myself that she seemed to be an excellent kind of girl for Traddles, too" (609; my emphasis; recall Schor's comment that a reference group is "a mental category, a comparison concept one carries around in one's head"). And not only must Dora be compared, in David's mind, to Sophy, but she must also be exhibited with Agnes, to the credit of both but the greater credit of the latter. "I never was so happy," writes David. "I never was so pleased as when I saw those two sit down together, side by side. As when I saw my little darling looking up so naturally to those cordial eyes. As when I saw the tender, beautiful regard which Agnes cast upon her" (617). Again like a distorting mirror, the comparison cuts both ways: Dora's instinctive admiration is itself admirable, but somehow less so because instinctive, and less so of course than that of Agnes, whose "regard" looks "down" while Dora's look looks up.

Other characters placed "side by side," in a by-no-means comprehensive list, are the deceased Mr. Copperfield and David's new stepfather; David and Steerforth ("comparing my merits with his" [309]); Steerforth and Mr. Meek; Steerforth and Ham; Mr. Meek and Mr. Creakle; Em'ly and Martha ("I was once like you" [345]; "comparing their departure [Ham and Em'ly] in my mind with Martha's" [350]). The difference between David and the other boys at Murdstone and Grinby's—"Though perfectly familiar with them, my conduct and manner were different enough from theirs to place a space between us" (172)—is countered by the "curious equality of friendship" he finds with the Micawbers, "originating, I suppose, in our respective circumstances" (173). (In this context, Mrs. Gummidge's claim to possess more misery than others defines her own economics of happiness.) Indeed, Rosa Dartle's relentless comparisons of David and Steerforth merely bring to the surface in sinister form the novel's business as usual, since what is noted is frequently noted solely because it suggests, "in David's mind," an interesting comparison with himself.

Differential Relations

It seems it should be Steerforth, with his elegant apartments, who sets the pace, who serves as model for all others. For what could be more Veblen-like than the dynamic of emulation and competition he acts out, as in the position at school that requires him, in his mother's words, to, "when it is his pleasure, outstrip every competitor" in a "spirit of emulation and conscious pride" (305). But emulation of Steerforth is not, of course, the novel's point, and its economics of happiness suggests why. Steerforth's, like Em'ly's, is the speculative version of happiness: that which must be preserved as a warning; that which the novel does not mean to endorse. David's own happiness in his friendship with Steerforth is thus expressed not in an imagining of likeness, but rather in a measuring of closeness to or distance from: happiness at school, for instance, lies in the belief that Steerforth "treated me in life unlike every other friend he had. I believed that I was nearer to his heart than any other friend, and my own heart warmed with attachment to him."

> A dashing way he had of treating me like a plaything, was more agreeable to me than any behaviour he could have adopted. It reminded me of our old acquaintance; it relieved me of any uneasiness I might have felt, in comparing my merits with his, and measuring my claims upon his friendship by any equal standard; above all, it was a familiar, unrestrained, affectionate demeanor that he used towards no one else. (309)

Like the Marmontel passage, the novel values not Steerforth's aristocratic brand of heroics but rather distinction within a familial and domestic field; it elevates over the aristocratic uniqueness of a Steerforth an ordinary boy who stands out amongst a group of others "like" himself. Since likeness to Steerforth cannot—and, in the novel's terms, should not—be David's goal, proximity must take its place, but that proximity differentiates even as it claims friendship. The idea that to desire a position as Steerforth's friend is to presume, to aim too high, bestows on Steerforth's careless treatment an equalizing effect; measurement, here as with happiness, makes it real. But David's apprehension of friendship as an anxious keeping of accounts, a balancing act in which potential slights are weighed against all-but-invisible signs of favor, belies his own claims for Steerforth's affection, the necessity of calculation defining rather what David's own culture might call an absence of friendship.

A rhetoric of measurement characterizes David's relations to others as well. Indeed, the novel is structured largely as a happiness competition, in which David's only true rivals are those who want what he wants. Hence the text's somewhat surprising magnification of small differences between David and the seemingly inconsequential Traddles, for instance—a friend who wants, but is permitted only a diminished version of, David Copperfield's own domestic bliss; and hence the intensity of the competition not between David and Steerforth but rather between David and Uriah, who not only wants the same kind of domesticity David does, but desires in fact the very same domesticity in the form of the very same wife. And here the domestic currency of happiness is mobilized once again. Just as Uriah is represented as a grotesque version of David, so too does the novel represent Heepian domesticity as an inversion—a "not at all" snug gesture toward the ideal.

> We entered and found a low, old-fashioned room, walked straight into from the street, and found there, Mrs. Heep, who was the dead image of Uriah, only short. She received me with the utmost humility, and apologised to me for giving her son a kiss, observing that, lowly as they were, they had their natural affections, which they hoped would give no offence to any one. It was a perfectly decent room, half parlor and half kitchen, but not at all a snug room. The tea-things were set upon the table, and the kettle was boiling on the hob. There was a chest of drawers with an escrutoire top, for Uriah to read and write at of an evening; there was Uriah's blue bag lying down and vomiting papers; there was a company of Uriah's books, commanded by Mr. Tidd; there was a corner cupboard; and there were the usual articles of furniture. I don't remember that any individual object had a bare, pinched, spare look; but I do remember that the whole place had. (264)

Uriah exemplifies not exactly unhappiness, but rather happiness's negative form, as if illustrating Bentham's hypothesis that what might be considered distinct emotions—pleasure and pain—are actually different sites along a continuum. Like David in ambition but absent all his good qualities, insincere where David is sincere and calculating where David is guileless, Uriah's focus on David's representation of happiness, David's domestic ideal, reinforces its universal quality as well as Uriah's own status as David's negative image: the reflection he will not see in his own mirror.[15]

For it is crucial to *David Copperfield*, as to Victorian domestic ideology in general, that situated as its characters' chief object of desire is not an object or some amount of money but rather a feeling, and the possibility of being a person—the kind of person—who can possess it. Indeed, this novel, like many other Victorian novels, structures identity as vicarious, positioning readers—like David—as heroes of their own lives: perhaps imagining themselves as rising characters; perhaps imagining that others will see them (as Mill imagines they might see him) as "everything" to everyone else. If Little Em'ly, in her desire to "feel more" and "be a better girl" reflects on the making of a happiness mistake, then, her error lies in her inability to avail herself of her culture's vicariousness: in being a character for whom the capacious term "happiness" is simply not capacious enough. Constructing her identity in relation to a particular conception of happiness—as Mill does when he asks whether his work will finally make him happy, or as David Copperfield does when he asks whether he will turn out to be the hero of his own life—she registers her knowledge that happiness is a representation in which she has failed to see herself. And yet her desire is not, specifically, to be happy, but rather to feel the things she knows she should feel—to fulfill the cultural imperative that wanting those things entails (as Mill writes, "To know that a feeling would make me happy if I had it, did not give me the feeling" [90])—in fact registers both happiness's status as compulsion (that which one must want) and her own transgressive desire, expressed here as a failure of vicariousness: the inability to find a mirror just the right size. Like her, many of the novel's characters are generally assessed and assess themselves not, exactly, in relation to what they want, but rather in relation to what they know they should want—if indeed these desires can be distinguished. For what one wants appears less compulsive, and less compulsory, when offered as a reward rather than required as a duty.

It is perhaps for this reason that, not so differently from but perhaps more fiercely than many Victorian novels, *David Copperfield*'s conclusion has about it a feeling not just of ending, but of winning—an indispensable element of the competitive society Veblen describes, and of the capitalist society whose terms Dickens no less than numerous others, including Trollope, transmutes into societal, and here, especially, familial ones. "Winning" is the term Uriah uses to describe his hopes for his relation to Agnes, and winning is what David, aided by Micawber, Mr. Dick, Aunt Betsey and others, succeeds in doing in relation to Uriah, that character so like him in ambition and yet so unlike him, the novel insists, in moral worth. (What has long struck readers as the fairy-tale quality of this novel—the way in which all those who block the hero's desires come to a bad end—is in fact characteristic of the structure of

Veblen's invidiousness: "a comparison of persons with a view to rating and grading them in respect of relative worth or value—in an aesthetic or moral sense—and so awarding and defining the relative degrees of complacency with which they may legitimately be contemplated by themselves and by others. An invidious comparison is a process of valuation of persons in respect of worth" [22]). Just as the Victorians notoriously sought to align money and morals, so too does *David Copperfield* tell us that those who win happiness must have deserved it (such is the circularity of Veblen's argument). Happiness in *David Copperfield*, and not just in *David Copperfield*, thus becomes the middle-class answer to money, offered as a salve for money's failures—especially, of course, its failure to turn up.

The image of happiness the novel most powerfully insists upon is, of course, the domestic scene realized at its end: the winning of Agnes, the company of loving family and friends. Writes David of the happiness moment that, among all the rest, is destined to be more than momentary: "I had advanced in fame and fortune; my domestic joy was perfect; I had been married ten happy years. Agnes and I were sitting by the fire, in our house in London, one night in spring, and three of our children were playing in the room, when I was told that a stranger wished to see me" (871). It is a scene coined in the linguistic currency of Victorian domestic ideology: "Perfect"; "happy"; "by the fire," "in our house."

"Ten happy years": the happiness moment is static, fixed, condensed in its assertion of longevity. Even the stranger's knock, which might differentiate this night from other nights, turns out to belong not to a stranger at all but to the now-displaced Peggoty, indicating—if there had been any doubt—that this is no happiness mistake, that David's achieved "interior" will return only positive reflections of him. But the novel's end also gestures briefly toward the way in which this achievement of happiness, the ostensible alignment of the real with the ideal, comes at the cost of a series of substitutions that reveal its exclusionary logic, taking shape as a fantasy of vicariousness in which the home David/Dickens desires is, both literally and figuratively, not just the home all others desire, but also the one (in his imagining of everyone else's imagining of him) "everyone" wishes him to have.[16] We see this in the detail, divulged by Agnes, that Dora requested her vacant place be filled only by Agnes herself; it is there as well in the echo of Dickens's own experience in David's brief allusion to the fact that the house Traddles's family moves into is one on which Traddles has long had his eye. Dickens, as is well known, lived from 1856 until his death in the home he had fixed on, as a child, as his future one.

> The house called Gadshill-place stands on the strip of highest ground
> in the main road between Rochester and Gravesend. Often we had trav-
> elled past it together, years and years before it became his home; and
> never without some allusion to what he told me when I first saw it in
> his company, that amid the recollections connected with his childhood
> it held always a prominent place, for, upon first seeing it as he came
> from Chatham with his father, and looking up at it with much admira-
> tion, he had been promised that he might himself live in it, or in some
> such house, when he came to be a man, if he would only work hard
> enough. Which for a long time was his ambition. (Forster I, 4)

Giving this accomplishment to Traddles rather than to David might seem
an instance of literary generosity—or perhaps a submerged acknowledgment that the fulfillment of yet another of David's childhood dreams
might try the affection of even the most indulgent of readers. But the
scenario in which you move into the house your childhood self dreamed
of inhabiting—a scenario that collapses the gap between the boy and
the man, as in the image of Mill reading Marmontel—neatly reverses
Mill's response to the happiness question, answering yes: were you to
get everything you wished for, you would be happy. Forster's "which" is
nicely ambiguous: is it Dickens's ambition to work hard, to earn his way
to the Gadshill house, or both; are these desires distinct, or a single one?
Representing his career, in this anecdote, as the successful fulfillment of
a childhood wish—a wish not surprisingly, given the domestic shape of
the cultural ideal this novel both defines and reinforces, to reside in his
own fantasy house—Dickens effectively closes a magic circle he himself
has opened. Working "hard enough," he fulfills his promise to himself—cashes in on the investment he has made in himself—and makes
good as well on his father's carefully contingent promise to him. Perhaps
most powerfully, the purchase of the house, defined as the fulfillment
of a childhood wish, effectively erases any fluctuations or divergences
that may have occurred along the way, except as they constitute fairy-
tale obstacles to a fairy-tale end. For unlike Mill, this narrative assures
us, Dickens got it right from the beginning, and rather than change his
notion of happiness he rearranged the world to provide it, rewriting it
on the model of the family with himself the beloved boy at its center.

Distant Reading

Moretti's Graph

Despite the now-commonplace deconstructive take on science and scientific authority in literary and cultural criticism, and despite work that points precisely in its direction—in sociology, statistics, and economic theory, by Canguilhem, Desrosières, Theodore Porter and Judy L. Klein, among others—the graph has tended to sail under the critical radar. Indeed, it has surfaced as an objective critical tool, the foundation for a new, scientifically oriented genre of literary criticism, in Franco Moretti's *Graphs, Maps, and Trees* (2001). Relying on graphs of novel publication to devise a new form of criticism based on scientific and statistical data, Moretti reproduces many of the effects I discuss throughout this book, projecting interiority onto external representations and mapping a personal trajectory onto an ostensibly historical one. Moretti's use of the graph serves as an example of the continued tendency to seek, in a way nineteenth-century science would have found familiar, reassurance in this figure's narrativity and readability.

Using the term "distant reading" to describe a literary analysis that relies on data rather than the close reading of texts, Moretti avers that any reading of novels in relation to graphs must replace a close focus on character, plot, and style with a dispassionate attention to details of publication history and numbers of readers: dispassionate, because the information obtained is not presumed to be in question. I have suggested throughout this book another meaning for the phrase "distant reading": one that finds distance not outside character but rather within it, the shaping of identity as an attachment to a series of consolidating abstractions. In Moretti's work, a search for objective data in the abstractions of genre and generation leads, not surprisingly, to a similar and similarly novelistic construction of identity.

Moretti proposes "a more rational literary history" (4). By "rational" he means founded on facts, or—the term he uses more frequently—"data." Neither science, sociology, or traditional literary criticism, the book is rather something like a literary sociology, using structures taken from "quantitative history, geography, and evolutionary theory" (1)—graphs, maps, and trees—to create visual models of "the literary field": models that will allow that field to be seen, literally and metaphorically, in a new way. An epigraph from Robert Musil's *Man without Qualities* points toward a certain instability in the genre to which the project belongs: "A man who wants the truth becomes a scientist; a man who wants to give free play to his subjectivity may become a writer; but what should a man do who wants something in between?" But Moretti's introduction, in contrast, describes:

> a new object of study: instead of concrete, individual works, a trio of artificial constructs—graphs, maps, and trees—in which the reality of the text undergoes a process of deliberate reduction and abstraction. 'Distant reading,' I have once called this type of approach; where distance is however not an obstacle, but a *specific form of knowledge:* fewer elements, hence a sharper sense of their overall interconnection. (1; emphasis in original)

Despite the Musil quotation, then, Moretti's language suggests that a result produced from "data"—one that ostensibly avoids the subjective effects of close reading by assuming a detached posture—does in fact rely on scientific authority: it will be, or will produce, "a specific form of knowledge." But in its use of and enthusiasm for the patterns revealed by graphs, the chapter recalls the work of nineteenth-century statisticians and social theorists such as Galton and Quetelet, who saw images of social harmony in the abstract regularity of mathematical forms and the symmetry of the graph's curve.

Moretti's analysis takes as its data information about the number of novels published from the early seventeen to the late eighteen hundreds: a larger number, he remarks, than familiar literary-critical modes would be capable of considering. If it is impossible even for this distant method—a simple tallying up—to account for such a vast number of books, however (as Moretti writes, "twenty thousand, thirty, no one really knows . . . " [4]), it is not, he claims, impossible to discern the structure of the system that underlies them. Demonstrating the existence of such a system involves attending not at the micro-level of words on the page but rather at the macro-level of publication data; the theory emerges from the graph, or series of graphs, constructed from these data.

What is the source of the information? Moretti frankly acknowledges the work of others, using statistics gathered by critics in Britain, India, Japan, Italy, Demark, and elsewhere.[1] "I mention these names right away," he writes, "because quantitative work is truly *cooperation:* not only in the pragmatic sense that it takes forever to gather the data, but because such data are ideally independent from any individual research-er, and can thus be shared by others, and combined in more than one way" (5; emphasis in original). And:

> Graphs are not really *models;* they are not simplified, intuitive versions
> of a theoretical structure in the ways maps and (especially) evolutionary
> trees will be in the next two chapters. Quantitative research provides a
> type of data which is ideally independent of interpretations. I said earlier,
> and that is of course also its limit: it provides *data,* not interpretation. . . .
> Quantitative data can tell us when Britain produced one new novel per
> month, or week, or day, or hour for that matter, but where the significant
> turning points lie along the continuum—and why—is something that
> must be decided on a different basis. (9; emphasis in original)

"Ideally independent," again: but this notion of the ideal is itself, in fact, the interpretation on which the graph, like the data found by Moretti's chosen researchers, is based. For a graph, like the data from which it is constructed, is not in fact independent of interpretation, but rather, precisely, a simplified, intuitive version "of a theoretical structure": it is a product of interpretation before any designated interpreter arrives on the scene. Someone chooses the data (what, for instance, will the category "novel" include?); someone plots the data (what period of time will the graph cover?); someone decides what shapes or variations are significant and worthy of further interpretation.

Moretti offers three possibilities for the structuring of historical nar-rative, based on Fernand Braudel's discussion of the *longue durée* of his-tory. He quotes Braudel:

> Traditional history, with its concern for the short time span, for the indi-
> vidual and the event, has long accustomed us to the headlong, dramatic,
> breathless rush of its narrative. . . . The new economic and social history

> puts cyclical movement in the forefront of its research . . . large sections
> of the past ten, twenty, fifty years at a stretch. . . . Far beyond this . . . we
> find a history capable of traversing even greater distances . . . to be
> measured in centuries . . . the long, even the very long time span, the
> *longue durée*. (13)

And comments thus: "The short span is all flow and no structure, the
longue durée all structure and no flow, and cycles are the—unstable—bor-
der country between them. Structures, because they introduce repetition
in history, and hence regularity, order, pattern; and temporary, because
they're short (ten, twenty, fifty years, this depends on the theory)" (14).
In other words, for the reader of graphs, what Moretti calls the "cycle"
offers a "just right" perspective: between a graph that would cover a
longue durée—perhaps the entire history of the novel—and one that
would detail changes so minute (publication by the second, or by the
hour) as to be, for Moretti's purposes, meaningless.

Moretti wants a pattern, because only a pattern will yield a theory.
He prefers a specific kind of pattern: one that appears only when data
included within a specific time-scheme are considered—not the longue
durée or the short, but one in-between. For only this intermediate period
yields the kinds of curves, or turns, that for him invite interpretation. Of
the appearance of two downward turns in a graph of novel publication
between 1775 and 1817, for instance, he writes,

> As possible causes multiply, one wonders: what are we trying to explain
> here—two *unrelated individual events,* or two moments *in a recurring pat-
> tern of ups and downs?* Because if the downturns are individual events,
> then looking for individual causes (Napoleon, reprints, the cost of paper,
> whatever) makes perfect sense; but if they are parts of a pattern, then
> what we must explain is *the pattern as a whole,* not just one of its phases.
> (13; emphasis in original)

The desired pattern is a "cycle," a series of recurring events or "temporary
structures." And here the argument makes a conceptual leap: what other
such structures are there? "Now, 'temporary structures' is also a good
definition for—genres," writes Moretti, "morphological arrangements
that *last* in time, but always only for *some* time" (14; emphasis in original).
How much time? According to Moretti, about twenty-five years.

> Janus-like creatures, with one face turned to history and the other to
> form, genres are . . . the true protagonists of this middle layer of literary

history—this more "rational" layer where flow and form meet. It's the regularity of figures 7 and 8 . . . with their three waves of epistolary novels from 1760 to 1790, and then gothic novels from 1790 to 1815, and then historical novels from 1815 to the 1840's. Each wave produces more or less the same number of novels per year, and lasts the same 25–30 years, and each also rises only after the previous wave has begun to ebb away. (14)

Why is 25–30 years a significant period? Not only does this length of time correspond, according to Moretti, to the rate at which one genre replaces another, but it also defines the period of time within which one human generation replaces another. In Moretti's Oedipally charged terms, "the decline of a ruling genre seems indeed here to be the necessary precondition for its successor's takeoff" (14). The generations at stake here are those of books and their readers; indeed, in a Darwinian explanation that ties the survival of the two together, he writes that "Books survive if they are read and disappear if they aren't: and when an entire generic system vanishes at once, the likeliest explanation is that *its readers vanished at once*" (20; emphasis in original).

Two necessary explanations: what is a generation, in the terms of Moretti's theory, and what a genre? Acknowledging that the "biological continuum" cannot be so precisely "segmented into discrete units," "since people are born every day, not every twenty-five years" (21), he relies on a definition of genre as a cultural formation: Karl Manheim's account of "generational style," which describes a generation as the result of a social and cultural process. "We shall therefore speak of a *generation as an actuality* only where a concrete bond is created between members of a generation by their being exposed to the social and intellectual symptoms of a process of dynamic destabilization" (emphasis in original). A generation is not just a life cycle, but an identity formation, the result of individuals perceiving themselves as culturally connected. As Moretti remarks, referring to his own generation, "one who was eighteen in 1968 understands" (21).

And what, in this argument, is a genre? For this category Moretti relies, as he did for his publication data, on the work of critics whose names and credits appear at the chapter's end. As is probably evident by now, the genre in question is not the novel, the graphing of which would not display the dramatic ups and downs Moretti seeks (though he provides a lovely, graphic literalization of the "rise" of the novel), but rather such classifications as the "courtship novel," the "picaresque," the "sentimental novel," the "spy novel," the "imperial gothic," and the "new woman" novel. Each category is accompanied by a citation to a work of literary criticism that either defines or gives a good account of it. Examples include: "Nautical Tales, 1828–50: Michael Wheeler, *English Fiction of the Victorian Period, 1830–90*, London 1985; Invasion Literature, 1871–14: I. F. Clarke, *The Tale of the Next Great War, 1871–1914*, Liverpool 1995; Nursery Stories, 1876–1906: Gillian Avery, *Nineteenth-Century Children*, London 1965" (32–33). This list, including as it does not just items called "novels" but also those designated as "tales," "stories," and "literature," creates an effect not unlike that of the classification of dissimilar items recounted in Borges's Chinese encyclopedia (discussed by Foucault in *The Order of Things*): a chaos that not only gestures toward the kind of inclusiveness of which Moretti despairs when he alludes to the impossibility of knowing exactly how many novels were published ("no one really knows . . . " [4]), but also undermines the notion of genre it has been created to support. "The mere act of enumeration that heaps them all together has a power of enchantment all its own," writes Foucault (*Order* xvi), but here the heap of terms attests more to the industriousness and creativity of literary critics working chiefly in the years between 1960 and 2000 than to the existence of secure literary classifications.

But even if one accepts Moretti's premise that the list does with some accuracy name novelistic genres, as Adena Rosmarin has pointed out, genres are not raw data but rather texts: evidence of "the constitutive power of our interpretative strategies," "pragmatic rather than natural; . . . used rather than described." Thus "there are precisely as many genres as we need, genres whose conceptual shape is precisely determined by that need. They are designed to serve the explanatory purpose of critical thought, not the other way around" (25). In terms that bear on Moretti's use of the graph to plot a particular kind of historical narrative, Rosmarin cites Hans Robert Jauss:

> Insofar as historical stories can be completed, can be given narrative closure, can be shown to have had a *plot* all along, they give to narrative reality the odor of the *ideal*. This is why the plot of a historical narrative is always an embarrassment and has to be presented as "found" in events rather than put there by narrative techniques. (37; emphasis in original)

Rosmarin's larger point is not that criticism should abandon genre as a conceptual category, but rather that critical argument can be strengthened by acknowledging the pragmatic nature of such classification, if only to defend against critiques on the subject: "By acknowledging rather than concealing its constitutive metaphors, it [the argument] anticipates and thus defends against their extramural deconstruction or unbuilding" (43). One might add to this that the establishing of genres in books and dissertations has its own history in literary-critical practice, not least as an identity-forming gesture, a way of marking differences between critical generations.

"The odor of the ideal" aptly describes the generational drama Moretti unearths in his cyclical pattern. For despite the skepticism with which he hedges his "findings," the data, and the shape of the graph constructed from them, for him possess the status of fact.

> "Variations in a conflict that remains constant": this is what emerges at the level of the cycle—and if the conflict remains constant, then the point is not who prevails in this or that skirmish, but exactly the opposite: no victory is ever definitive, neither men nor women writers "occupy" the British novel once and for all, and the form keeps oscillating back and forth between the two groups. And if this sounds like nothing is happening, no, what is happening *is the oscillation,* which allows the novel to use a double pool of talents and of forms, thereby boosting its own productivity, and giving it an edge over its many competitors. But this process can be glimpsed *only at the level of the cycle:* individual episodes tend, if anything, to conceal it, and *only the abstract pattern reveals the true nature of the historical process.* (29; emphasis in original)

Novel history, then, is defined here as a recurrent cycling of genres, in which what matters chiefly is not any particular genre but the process or "oscillation" that "allows the novel to use a double pool of talents and of forms, thereby boosting its productivity, and giving it an edge over its many competitors. But this process can only be glimpsed *at the level of the cycle:* individual episodes tend, if anything, to conceal it, and only the abstract pattern reveals the true nature of the historical process." What Moretti suggests he has discovered, in other words, is the "hidden tempo" or "internal shape" of novel history: a historical "form" of which individual novels or genres are the "substance" (29). This notion of form borrows from, without specifically invoking, the idea of novel form—detaching it from individual novels and situating it in historical time; reifying it in the abstract pattern made visible by a graph.

Moretti is unable to locate a pattern in the data, the numbers, the names of genres—nor can he offer an analysis, transform them into theory, or perceive their "beauty"—until he represents them in the form of a graph. Only then does he begin to perceive "phases" and "cycles"; only then does he begin to construct—or, as he puts it, perceive—the "hidden" truth of the historical process. The graph makes regularity out of chaos—or rather, in Moretti's repeated term, reveals the regularity hidden within chaos. And, I would argue, the apparent confirmation of these "truths" lies in the way the 25-year pattern he perceives seems to literalize, or vivify, what had until that point been "only" a metaphor (as in "the rise of the novel"). For despite Moretti's appeal to Manheim's cultural idea of generation, what the graph appears in this argument to support, and seems to render in visible terms, is the publication data's overlap with what is for Moretti not only an inarguable biological process, but also a generational drama and emotional cycle in which genres appear as characters, or "protagonists" (14). "From individual cases to series; from series to cycles, and then to genres as their morphological embodiment. And these three genres seem indeed to follow a rather regular 'life-cycle,' as some economists would call it. These genres—or *all* genres? Is this wave-like pattern a sort of hidden pendulum of literary history?" (18; emphasis in original).

What then, is "more rational" about Moretti's literary history? "Quantitative data can tell us when Britain produced one new novel per month, or week, or day, or hour for that matter," he argues, "but where the significant turning points lie along the continuum—and why—is something that must be decided on a different basis" (9). But *that* there are "significant turning points" is never in doubt: there is no question for Moretti that the graph is "already" a narrative whose meaning it is the critic's job to discern. "As possible causes multiply, one wonders: what are we trying to explain here—two *unrelated events*, or two moments *in a recurring pattern of ups and downs?*" It is never clear when, or why, that question is answered as it is answered here: why "what we must explain is *the pattern as a whole*, not just one of its phases" (13; emphasis in original). But in discerning a pattern in the graph, and reading that pattern as a generational drama, Moretti makes use of a strategy that mirrors Galton's: both apply to human society the abstract truths or mathematical "laws" that seem to be revealed when certain data are plotted on a graph. Rationality here turns out to refer to a rationalization of the social order: the idea, that is, that some law or rule underlies and regulates human activity (the wave metaphor further suggests the naturalness and inevitability of a pattern).

As Galton's and Quetelet's use of the error law reveals, the representation of the actions and identities of numerous, multifarious individuals as a system—the cause of some pattern—is the result of elimination and abstraction, the transformation of data into a mathematical form which may, then, reveal a mathematical truth. (Recall Quetelet's description of the perfect circle that can only be discerned from a distance.) But an attempt to return to the supposed source of the data—reading that abstraction back into human identity and human social forms—will discover not truth but rather the ideality offered by the system itself. The novel and the graph offer overlapping and mutually-reinforcing imaginative vehicles for ruling the unruly and rendering the unclear clear, most particularly in the arena of human emotion; they also serve as mechanisms of transformation, assimilating dissimilar elements within a single framework, most appealingly that of character. For Moretti, the graph transforms data about publication and genre into cycles, which he then ties to the cycle of generations. But the assumption that patterns perceived in one place are connected to patterns perceived in another owes less to any kind of "rational" evidence, here, than it does to a mapping of social processes onto natural ones.

Moretti is not the first critic, of course, to assimilate literary generations to familial ones, and his argument is to some degree a Bloomian one; indeed, it is not clear what his brand of rationality adds to Harold Bloom's account of generational replacement. But even as Moretti acknowledges his inability to explain in definitive terms what the data mean, he offers an illustrative account of the kinds of questions that tend to be asked—the kinds of features or elements that become visible as objects of interest—when the answer takes shape as a graph.

> Now, let me be clear, saying that these studies describe the return of the same literary cycle is not an objection: quite the opposite, my thesis *depends* on their findings, and it even corroborates them somehow, by finding the common mechanism which is at work in all these instances. But it's also true that *if one reframes individual instances as moments of a cycle*, then the nature of the questions changes: "Events don't interest Lucien Febvre for what in them is unique," writes Pomian, but "as units in a series, which reveal the conjectural variations in . . . a conflict that remains constant throughout the period." Variations in a conflict that remains constant: this is what emerges at the level of the cycle. . . . (27; emphasis in original)

To return to the novel, then, and to the other literal and metaphorical graphs discussed in my earlier chapters: though individual instances may be framed as "moments of a cycle," that is not the only possible way of framing them; the "conjectural variations in . . . a conflict that remains constant" also describes the interest of, for instance, the difference between speculators and investors; the distance of individual characters from the average man; the question of how much happiness an individual may be said to have. Variations are of interest only insofar as the specific conflict to which they belong is not itself interrogated; only when the pattern is in place do variations become visible as that which deserves attention and rewards scrutiny. Moretti's cycles, in other words, define as discovery and historical truth what is necessarily of interest to a student of the graph: those variations within a *longue durée* that have some meaning for the life-trajectory of the average man. Only in those variations is it possible to discern the outlines of a self and the generation to which he belongs.

The Graph as Novel

The figure of the graph echoes, even as it invites, the construction of novelistic narrative, while novelistic narrative also invites the imagining of a graph, a variety of inchoate material translated—so that it can be read, comprehended, managed—into characters, emotions, and identities. Indeed, the identification of emotion as a kind of currency (as in the "fear index" that began to make news in 2009) enables the stock market to function today—as it did as soon as the rise and fall of share prices began to reverberate in the consciousnesses of large numbers of people in the nineteenth century—as the emotional barometer of the average man. The term "average," here as throughout my argument, refers not to an ostensibly accurate mathematical or scientifically arrived-at consensus, but rather, as in the case of Pancks's wooden-leggedness, to the referral of information about the self to one's idea of someone else—indeed, of multiple someone elses—whose situations and identities seem, within the terms of a particular cultural narrative, comparable to one's own.

Graphs serve as representations of collective feeling in other areas as well. In his 2006 film *An Inconvenient Truth,* for instance, Al Gore dramatized the threat of global warming by riding a cherry-picker alongside a giant graph—the image externalizing, as he proposed the climate itself does, a planetary "nervous system" (a dramatic gesture that reinforces Marita Sturken's analysis of weather observation as a mechanism of national or global cohesion, and resonates with Terry Castle's description of the way the barometer registers an imagined correspondence between internal and external "weather"). Like happiness; like the stock-market graph, Gore's figure for climate change assimilates innumerable, uncoordinated details and events to a single, evidently simple, persuasively elegant trajectory. Representing the earth's future as a line soaring to unknown heights, Gore's graph suggests that the solid foundation once granted by the average has given way to the anxious tracking of our collective distance from it. Scientific representation, at least in this instance, is unproblematically assimilated to and rendered indistinguishable from emotional projection.

Or: viewers of the 2008 Presidential debates on CNN witnessed, in addition to the images of the candidates themselves, a "screen crawl" displaying the responses of a group of "undecided" voters. Those responses, transmitted by pressure exerted on hand-held devices, were then assimilated to a graph, with lines divided in color according to gender. Thus issued a running commentary, delivered to viewers in the flattened rhetoric of the graph. The episode exemplifies the kind of ideological condensation I have discussed throughout this book: the unquestioned assumption that the graph captures and transmits an unmediated emotional response. Indeed, the very category of the undecided voter draws on the idea of the average as a mediator between two extremes, the graph literalizing an emotional balance that responds with a hair-trigger sensitivity to a candidate's every inflection. Like the stock-market graph, this figure structures voting as an emotional investment, positioning viewers as effects of its collective narrative. Tracking the candidates' voices, movements, and expressions, observers (not now financial investors, but rather political ones) become subjects of its simplifying trajectory.

The historicizing or contextualization of emotion often relies on an already constituted object: instead of asking how the term "happiness" acquired the consolidating effect it possesses, for example, the tendency is to ask how happiness was represented or constituted in any given historical period. I have attempted here not to trace the history of any particular emotion or indeed of the figure of the graph, but rather to suggest the ways in which a habit of quantification ties the Victorian novel to both Victorian and modern systems of representation, borrowing an aura of scientific authority to create social realities and establish emotional currencies as coherent categories for understanding the self. The readings offered here outline a generally unacknowledged continuity between the Victorian novel and the graph as vehicles that promote the tracking of what appears as a coherent stream of feeling, facilitating an apparently successful, because apparently coherent, mapping of interiority. And the project as a whole underscores the way in which despite a widespread critique of scientific representation, the figure of the graph and the conceptual grid it exemplifies have generally escaped cultural studies' notice: an especially surprising omission in Victorian Studies, given persistent interest in the period's constructions of scientific authority.

To characterize an individual's relation to him or herself as a function of distant reading might seem to conjure up ideas of self-estrangement or self-alienation. My argument is rather that terms commonly associated with and assigned to the arena of personal life—emotion-designating terms such as happiness or, to use an example recently taken up by Christopher Lane, shyness—are in the first place descriptions of collective identity, naming a fantasmatic coherence in relation to which individuals position themselves. This is partly an effect of normalizing influences exerted throughout Victorian culture via discourses such as medicine, statistics, or, as Timothy Alborn has shown, the requirements of the insurance industry. But more generally, the inscription of the self within any collective cultural narrative requires distant reading: the evaluation of one individual's position in relation to that construction; an apprehension of the self as both participating in and differing from a consolidated and coherent image of the whole. The graph thus illuminates the Victorian novel, which in turn illuminates the graph, both possessing the aesthetic and emotional coherence that enable them to function as vehicles for ideology, the beauty of the pattern acting as a guarantee of whatever meaning is attributed to it. That same power inheres in the concept of character itself, in which innumerable aspects of identity, assimilated to a limited number of forms or trajectories— variations on the average—produce compelling, ideologically satisfying narratives.

Or again: to say that the Victorian novel plays a role in helping us read distantly might seem at odds with traditional notions of the novel's value—with the richness of detail that informs novelistic representations of character. But to see that richness of detail as a necessary response to the smoothing and normalization of character at work throughout Victorian culture provides another context for the idea of individuality itself: one already recognized and widely discussed in the context of other ideologies and classifications. It is also to suggest that Victorian novels in tandem with other discourses of identity and emotion habituated readers to certain kinds of narrative structures—producing and reinforcing an investment in character as an explanatory device. The consequence of failing to see this tendency as historical is a certain diversion of attention from, for example, what might be seen as flaws in or failures of a system to a recognizable and therefore comforting narrative.

The juxtaposition of Victorian and contemporary materials throughout this book differs, therefore, from the emphasis on recovery that has prevailed in Victorian studies since the advent of the New Historicism, as well as from the kind of obsession or fascination with Victorian life and Victorian things characteristic of what Cora Kaplan has called "Victoriana." Indeed, rather than following up the issue of the self-conscious appropriation of the past, this book is about unselfconscious appropriation: the persistent, often unacknowledged shaping of twentieth- and twenty-first century daily life by structures of narrative and character shaped and disseminated by the Victorian novel. This persistence is visible, I have argued, in the kinds of stories we continue to tell about the community, but it exists as well in contemporary narratives about the measurement of happiness, in which an idea of happiness as being obviously different from and better than money, but also somehow remarkably similar to it (an effect that appears not least in the need to compare the two) makes more sense in the context of its Victorian genealogy. Conditioned by Victorian narrative and especially by a novelistic emphasis on character, a reflexive noting of the ups and down of the market takes shape in popular discourse and in the visceral responses of stock-market subjects as an attribution of emotion and intention to a series of abstractions. Reliance on such narratives, and especially on character as an explanatory device, makes sense of the otherwise inexplicable workings of the stock market, resolving innumerable satisfactions and dissatisfactions, likes and dislikes, potentialities and obstacles into a definition of the collective self as happy or not happy.

The benefit of finding in contemporary discourse a Victorianism we didn't know was there in the form of an obeisance to the supposed exigencies of character—a characterological narrative of everyday life—may simply be that awareness itself, along with a renewed appreciation of the persistence of this particular historical narrative. But it may also provide cultural criticism with a new object of analysis in the figure of the graph, and a new mode of analysis directed not toward uncovering the significance of particular ups and downs—as in the "mood" of the economy or the nation—but rather toward the pervasive tendency to personify such abstractions, inviting us to ask why we make the graph into a character and what our continuing investment in doing so might be.

NOTES

INTRODUCTION

1. One might also adduce the effect on Galton of not-too-distant events in English politics, such as the Hyde Park riots, that drew attention to the "unruliness" of at least a portion of England's population. It was Galton, after all, whose attention to bodily irregularities—the curves and whorls that furrow our fingertips—helped facilitate the police work of the modern state, hailing the uniqueness of each individual so that innumerable and diverse fingerprints could be marshaled into innumerable government files.

2. Of the modern emphasis on numerical representation, Mary Poovey writes that "to assign numbers to observed particulars is to make them amenable to the kind of knowledge system that privileges quantity over quality, equivalence over difference." Pam Morris discusses the "technologies and protocols [that] facilitate the process of abstraction whereby differences of class, gender, region, and race are homogenized into a mass consumer culture" (Poovey, *Fact* 4; Morris 6).

3. Since the rise of affect theory, defining the difference between "affect," "feeling," and "emotion" has become something of a cottage industry. Since I am concerned with the way such reifications come into being, I do not engage that discussion here.

4. The new economic criticism is no longer so new, and includes a substantial body of work. Aside from the books by Gallagher and Poovey noted above, see Klaver, Houston, and Woodmansee and Osteen.

5. For Silverman, this is also an Althusserian argument about interpellation: she discusses Althusser's reconception of the mirror stage as "something that occurs on a mass as well as an individual level" (24).

6. Critical discussions of the nineteenth-century emphasis on quantification include Anne McClintock's account of the rationalization of household activity and Cathy Shuman's work on the application of rational techniques in education, especially 1–19. Though Nancy Armstrong's *Fiction in the Age of Photography* focuses on a different kind of image, her analysis accurately describes the more general system of representation I discuss here.

Though she is concerned with the way twentieth-century American surveys create a sense of a mass public, Sarah Igo discusses the assimilation of the many into a coherent, average unit in ways that reflect my concerns. "The drive to determine the average was part empirical quest, part cultural preoccupation," she writes. . . . "In 1947, for example, *Newsweek* could announce that there was a 'shadowy figure beginning to emerge' from the day's public opinion polls, which it promptly labeled the 'American Majority Man.' Such composite types, placeholders for the nation itself, flowed easily from scientific tables and graphs. . . . This figment of surveyors' imaginations could work to highlight and regulate differences, permitting individuals not only to discern an aggregate norm but also to measure themselves against it . . . " (*The Averaged American* 20–21). My emphasis is not on the historical construction of the idea of the average, but rather on the way in which—from the tables and graphs to the shadowy figure that emerges from them—every step of the process is a figment of someone's imagination.

7. My discussion of Sarah Ahmed's work, below, is relevant here as well.

8. Frances Ferguson notes the connection between the novel as a form and the social sciences in a discussion of Austen's *Emma:* "A communal contribution enables us to recognize Emma as good even when she is not. Its voicing in free indirect style taps into the approach of the social sciences that allows us (and direct marketing firms) to see that someday we may well do what many people roughly like us would do. . . . This narrative approach shares a deep affinity with the basic procedures of the social sciences, which project a time line and a series of prophecies for individuals less from their own histories than from an analysis of the group" (164–65). And Armstrong has written about the "undertheorized" nature of "the figure of mass man" in a discussion of repetition (*How Novels Think* 113).

9. A few recent studies have addressed the emergence of the figure of the "mass" in Victorian discourse: see Seltzer, Plotz, and Armstrong (*How Novels Think*). Rather than discussing the "mass" as a threatening "other" whose image must be expunged—what Armstrong calls "phobic representations of the human aggregate" (25)—I argue that nineteenth-century representations of individual identity necessarily emerge as effects of identification with images of an aggregate or mass man. For other discussions of group emotion, see Brennan, Plotz, and Williams, "Moving Pictures." Peter Logan discusses group emotion briefly (*Nerves and Narratives*).

10. Poovey writes, "[T]he conventions professional social scientists use to connect the large scale to particulars are based on mathematical principles, and this tends to bolster the authority of social scientists . . . statistical sampling is a mathematically based method that grounds generalizations about 'populations' on small numbers of observations, and the concept of a 'social fact' helps substantiate claims about numerically demonstrable regularities even when personal experience seems to contradict these claims." Professionalized social science, argues Poovey, is made possible by "general agreement among practitioners about the conventions and methods that are necessary for scientific validity" ("Structure of Anxiety" 159–60). See also Klein, Canguilhem, and Porter.

11. My assumptions about the construction of the self rely, as my discussion of Kaja Silverman's work above suggests, on Foucauldian and Althusserian models: on the idea of the subject as an effect of representational regimes. I do not, however,

argue that the self thereby produced is singular, unitary, or wholly determined, but am instead in agreement with, for example, arguments by Rei Terada and others in which subjectivity appears inherently divided. When I use the term "individual," as I do throughout this book, it is with an awareness that nineteenth-century representations often figure individual identity as it emerges from, or may be seen in contrast with, an undifferentiated mass or crowd.

12. Jonathan Crary writes in similar terms that, in the nineteenth century, photography and money are both "magical forms" sanctioned by "consent": forms that "establish a new set of abstract relations between individuals and things and impose those relations as the real" (13). And Susan Buck-Morss writes similarly about economics: "The discovery of the economy was also its invention. . . . The great marvel is that once a scientific object is discovered (invented) it takes on agency. The economy is now seen to act in the world; it causes events, creates effects" (116). See also the idea of the "real" in Desrosières, for instance 70 and 82.

13. The familiar mathematical average—in which numbers are added together and then divided—is the best-known example of the kind of synthetic construction I discuss throughout this book, but it is not the only example. The term "average" refers in general to synthetic or cohesive representations that function as reference points in relation to which other terms acquire meaning; like the term "normal," it has specific uses in different disciplines as well as an ideological use based on some agreed-upon notion of a scientific consensus. No individual possesses an "average" heartbeat, for instance; the pace of any particular heartbeat is meaningful only in comparison with a fictional construct, an idea of an average. Similarly, a stock price is not a mathematical average—the result of multiple transactions added up and then divided—but rather a number representing the net effect of numerous transactions, evaluated in relation to a selected starting point. Canguilhem's work is especially useful in suggesting the many uses to which the idea of the average has been put and the variety of disciplinary sites in which averages may be located. He discusses the ideas of the "typical" and the "mathematical" average in Quetelet's work, as well as the relation between a biological average and a social one in *The Normal and the Pathological* 157–58 and 160–61. Canguilhem writes, for instance, that "[W]hen we speak of an average life, in order to show it growing gradually, we link it to the action that man, taken collectively, exercises on himself . . . [thus] the average life span is not the biologically normal, but in a sense the sociologically normative, life span. Once more the norm is not deduced from, but rather expressed in the average. This would be clearer still if, instead of considering the average life span in a national society taken as a whole, we broke this society down into classes, occupations, etc." (161).

14. For an extended discussion of Bertillon, see Sekula.

15. Contemporary face-recognition technology uses roughly the same approach, relying on composite structures called "eigenfaces."

16. Armstrong also describes this relationship as a struggle: "The early Lacan allows us to imagine just how culturally disseminated images might have entered into that individual's development by providing a self-image he could either replicate or violate, but with which he had to struggle for a lifetime either way" (*Fiction* 25).

17. "Quetelet even proposed a theory of the enlightened will to explain the greater regularity of moral statistics than those of births and deaths. It involved, in effect, a will to mediocrity, a tendency for the enlightened to resist the influences of external circumstances and to seek always to return to a normal and balanced state" (Porter, *Rise* 103).

18. For a discussion of the average in Quetelet's work as an expression of the socially normative, see Canguilhem 156–62.

19. "According to Walter Bagehot, who began to write for the paper in 1857, the *Economist* launched 'the economic age,' for it was a great 'belief producer' that made the members of the growing middle class feel like they belonged to a single, if complex, community" (Poovey, *Financial System*, 26). The term "imagined community" is Benedict Anderson's. Houston writes that the "business cycle" has "tremendous repercussions on the quality of emotional, psychological, and physical life. . . . I assume that words have the power to produce biological actions and reactions in the human body" (10). Rather, accounts of such responses are a crucial component of stock-market representation and rhetoric: the chief means by which the market is naturalized, its "movement" aligned with that of the social and individual body.

20. Ahmed discusses the attribution of feeling to collectives such as nations (13). The stock market offers a striking example of a system that ties emotion to numbers in a culture in which money, as a vehicle for self-representation and self-evaluation, has already rendered identity, and any system of numbers that purports to represent it, fungible.

21. These are not examples of "homo economicus"—the rational man posited by economic theory—but rather projections of the market.

This book was begun in the late 1990s and early 2000s, inspired, at the end of the dot-com boom, by a wish to understand the stock-market's role as an emotional mirror from the Victorian period to the present day. Events of late 2008 and early 2009 bring another such cycle to an end. But if updating particular sections by changing names—even as, in December 2008, the financial universe offers the gift of another "M" name (why always M?) to form the triad of Merdle, Melmotte, and Madoff—seems unnecessary, the possibility of doing so demonstrates, first, the ways in which the emotional investments of Victorian and contemporary stock-market subjects and the scenarios that compel them remain unchanged, and second, as I argue more fully below, the way the stock market and the Victorian novel function as mutually constructing, mutually reinforcing discourses. Thus if, for Patricia Cohen, Bernard Madoff is another in a series of fraudulent financier-characters whose actions blur the boundaries between the fictional and the real, this is because what Paul Krugman calls, with respect to Madoff, "the investment industry" tends repeatedly to be cast within the narrative and characterological terms of Victorian fiction. Thus Madoff's actions quickly become a "story" that makes the most sense when viewed through the lens of the Victorian novel—that makes sense, indeed, only when viewed as a Victorian novel. In particular, such stories stabilize the possibility I discuss in chapter 2: the anxiety that there may be no logic to or rationale behind the market's scenarios of winning and losing. The most threatening thing about the stock market, that is, may be the irrelevance to it of moral categories: a meaninglessness both exposed and apparently mitigated by the drama of fraud (see Krugman and Cohen).

22. Soni traces a transition from a pre-eighteenth century, communal notion to a modern sense of happiness as "individual, private, affective satisfaction" (15, 18).

23. Her most prominent example involves the idea of national mourning: "To say, 'the nation mourns' is to generate the nation, *as if it were a mourning subject*" (13). The same may be said for descriptions of the stock market as nervous or depressed; in both cases, the collective subject generated by the phrase creates the emotion and makes it available for identification.

24. Gallagher points out that "Bentham never successfully negotiated the psychological gap between particular felicific calculations and general ones, which is why he came to rely on the government to close it" (*Body Economic* 69).

25. For a discussion of continuities between Victorian and modern culture, especially in economics, see Kucich and Sadoff on "the nineteenth century as the originary site of our economic situation." Citing Giovanni Arrighi's work on capitalism, Kucich and Sadoff suggest that "[I]n the postmodern imaginary . . . the 'break' between economic production and economic reproduction, between technologies of manufacture and technologies of the production and control of value itself, becomes a key to understanding the relationships among nationalism, industrialism, and technological development" (xvii).

CHAPTER ONE

1. These comments are made by different characters, chief among them Mr. Brooke, who is central to Eliot's ventriloquizing of the Middlemarch point of view. But as I discuss further below, the narrator is also a frequent user of the term "like" and the comparative mode it signifies, and my blurring together of different voices is intentional. Eliot's interest in the problem of the "mass" resemblance of individuals to one another is addressed in Lynch 251, Cottom, and Woloch. Woloch discusses the way the novel suggests an "imperative to look at the masses of 'ordinary life' and [at the same time] anxiously worries that the sight might be too much" (32).

2. Accounts of the development of statistics in the nineteenth century and beyond can be found in Porter, *Statistical Thinking;* Stigler; and Poovey, *Fact.* Discussions of the political use of statistics can be found in Porter, *Trust* and in Desrosières.

3. For an opposing view, see Gallagher, "Immanent Victorian."

4. "Endowed with every virtue, Quetelet's 'average man' was presented as a kind of prudent centrist, who avoided every conceivable form of excess—for perfection lies in moderation" (Desrosières, 79).

5. Mark Seltzer approaches the phenomenon of the statistical person from a different perspective; in his view, the serial killer is "the very icon of the mass in person" (*Serial Killers,* 7).

6. Or rather, a kind of figure, for Quetelet imagined not just one average man but many; "there would be an average man at each age, of each race, in each country, and at each combination of these" (Stigler 171).

7. The real is an important category for Desrosières; he uses the term to refer to "a ground for action." "Statistical tools allow the discovery or creation of enti-

ties that support our descriptions of the world and the way we act on it. Of these objects, we may say both that they are real and that they have been constructed, once they have been repeated in other assemblages and circulated as such, cut off from their origins—which is after all the fate of numerous products. . . . The question of reality is linked to the solidity of this system, and its ability to resist criticism. The more extensive and dense it is, the more reality it has" (3).

8. This is another way of describing one of the mechanisms that makes the process of Althusserian interpellation possible: how it can be that multiple, individual subjects of a given society can also identify, as a group, with certain elements of that society. In this account, the average is absorbed into each individual's "sense" of identity but does not wholly constitute it. Any individual is thus less an "identity" than a manager of identities, capable of sustaining many different identities at once. Such a construction makes it possible, for instance, to suspend critical judgment about, or disdain for, the average, or to participate in an "average" activity without wholly identifying with it: to want what others want and buy what others buy, for instance, without a sense that individual identity is thereby compromised.

9. Wolloch argues that the nineteenth-century novel regularly presents a series of compelling minor characters in competition with major ones for novelistic space and readerly attention, and he cites this passage to demonstrate that "Mayhew's graphic image maps social deviance to a specific class of individuals" (163). But this reading overlooks the passage's rich personality calculus: its description of a "many" less in competition with the one than inhabiting him.

10. This is a version of what Wolloch and others, most famously Lukacs, call a "type": "How do you represent ten people who share the same living conditions, or ten thousand people who all belong to the same social class? You can find common traits and conjure up a single individual who exemplifies much more widespread characteristics" (Wolloch, 249).

11. Useful here is another definition of the real, to accompany that of Desrosières: Ian Hacking's idea of "dynamic nominalism," according to which the invention of a category invites people to locate themselves within it, thus generating new forms of behavior and new identities.

12. For an example of likeness anxiety, one need only assess the tone of the novel's "Finale," in which readers learn that Dorothea's fate is to be "only known in a certain circle as a wife and mother," one of those "who lived faithfully a hidden life, and rest in unvisited tombs" (895–96). Such passages convey the feeling that, for Eliot, "to be obscure is not to be" (Bedient, 86).

13. For a further discussion of Quetelet's aestheticism, see Sekula.

14. Or, more precisely, the description works by taking away what it has oh-so-grudgingly given: that hint of individuality—perhaps feeling of superiority—present in Mary's expression. You too, reader, may imagine yourself an individual, but the novel reminds you, even as you identify with Mary's secret, of your mass status: your membership in a group of others like yourself. Not simply subjecting readers to the pressures of statistical likeness, that "ten-to-one" keeps them slightly off balance as well.

15. In a contemporary example of the same phenomenon, covers of the June 2004 issue of *Reason* magazine pictured aerial portraits of subscribers' homes and neighborhoods. The featured essay, "Database Nation," by Declan McCullagh,

argues that present-day consumers are well-served by the collection of information about them: by such inventions as supermarket discount cards, for instance, which transmit information about their users. In the context of such databases—about neighborhoods, consumer tastes, and political leanings, among other things—the individual figures as a function of a statistical representation of the mass or the group: someone "like" himself.

16. On medicine's relation to statistics, see Hacking, ch. 6; on the use of averages in relation to the "normal" in medicine, see Canguilhem. For instance: "In order to represent a species we have chosen norms which are in fact constants determined by averages. The normal living being is the one who conforms to these norms. But must we consider every divergence abnormal?" (154).

17. This double movement—an identification with the wavering line, rather than with a fixed position—is an effect of Eliot's attempt simultaneously to reproduce the affective quality of middle-class consciousness and to look at it from the outside, where (like Lydgate) she locates herself.

18. The idea of "equivalence" is crucial to Jevons's economics. "Jevons rightly argued that there were in fact no numbers needed at all. Just as someone could roughly perceive the equilibrium of a balance with the eye, so the individual was able to judge the equivalence of pleasures and pains by paying attention only to their marginal increase or decrease. No assumption was needed as to whether the mind was able to judge accurately numerical quantities of utility. It was only necessary to assume that the mind could perceive a rough equivalence (or inequality) between them" (Maas 296).

19. "Now, the only dimension belonging properly to feeling seems to be *intensity*, and this intensity must be independent both of time and of the quantity of commodity enjoyed. . . . Intensity of feeling . . . is only another name for the degree of utility which represents the favourable effect produced upon the human frame by the consumption of commodity" (65). And this: "The intensity of present anticipated feeling must, to use a mathematical expression, increase as we approach the moment of realization" (34).

CHAPTER TWO

1. I take the term and the concept from Arlie Russell Hochschild.

2. Ahmed discusses the way "subjects become invested in particular structures" and attribute emotion to objects such as nations. "Emotions provide a script, certainly: you . . . accept the invitation to align yourself with the nation"; To say 'the nation mourns' is to generate the nation, as if it were a mourning subject. The 'nation' becomes a shared 'object of feeling' through the orientation that is taken towards it" (12–13). Sometimes the terms "speculators" or "speculation" refer to a reified abstraction, sometimes to a group of people buying and selling stocks and shares. Terms such as "panic" and "mania" slide between the two. For a nineteenth-century example of the use of such characterizations, see Shand, "Speculative Investments" (1876) in Poovey, *Financial Systems* 173–76.

3. "Sparked by the dramatic growth in stock investment in the early part of the decade, writing about financial issues began to be a regular part of London and provincial newspapers in the 1820s. Unlike the dry tables of market informa-

tion previously published, however, this new financial journalism treated the City as a distinct culture, which writers assumed would be intrinsically interesting to readers" (Poovey, *Financial System* 28).

4. I am thinking here of Cvetkovich's work on sensation and affect and Gallagher, *The Body Economic*. Neither discusses the relation between the stock market, emotion, and the body. In *Nerves and Narratives*, Logan cites Thomas Trotter's discussion of the way the stock exchange "has filled the nation with degenerate fears, apprehension, and hypochondriacism"; the cause of this, suggests Logan, is the "web of mutual dependencies" that defines a credit economy (32–33).

5. Writes Michie, "Options were and remained an essential but unrecognized aspect of dealing in securities" (50).

6. It was necessary "to exclude those who were untrustworthy, because of past actions or present reputation, or [those who] created risks for other members, due to their additional activities" (Michie 38).

7. My claim is not, of course, that these terms came into existence with the Victorian novel, but rather that during the period they came to be understood less as roles one played in the stock market—as, for instance, they were in the eighteenth century—and more as psychological complexes, keys to character as a whole. Garrett Ziegler notes that the importance bestowed by Victorian novels on "the funds, the five percents, and the stock market, as well as the more pernicious elements of the new economy, like debt, fraud, and bankruptcy[. These] offer a thorough, if slightly disproportionate, sense of the movement toward capitalization and its attendant concerns . . . the vast majority of Britons during the nineteenth century had no savings to speak of and were generally not interested or able to participate in the burgeoning culture of investment." But "by 1850 nearly forty percent of all assets held by British citizens were financial, according to Michie . . . so even if the average Victorian never conferred with a broker or was taken in by a speculator, he or she would have been quite conscious of the world of the Exchange, especially during the tumultuous 1850's" (Ziegler 434).

8. Jonathan Freedman, discussing Friedrich Hayek's work, writes, "The mechanism by which the marketplace sets its prices is a form of thought; the price of things is a means by which millions of people communicate information to each other with super-rational speed and efficiency" (*The Temple of Culture* 63). But prices are averages, not actual representations of what "millions of people"are doing, nor are those people communicating with one another. Any "communication" about value is mediated through the representation of prices and of the market in which they circulate. The idea of price here has more in common with the fantasmatic idea of an emotional barometer, of "fluctuations . . . powerfully internalized [because] they have come to register the ineluctable psychopathology of everyday life" (Castle 40).

9. See Reed, "A Friend to Mammon."

CHAPTER THREE

1. This chapter was begun toward the end of the "boom" of the late 1990s: before its end was officially designated. But what was then called the "slow down" of winter 2000–01 was a slow down only in the context of the bubble narrative. Writes Robert Shiller: "The present stock market displays the classic features of

a speculative bubble, a situation in which temporarily high prices are sustained largely by investors' enthusiasm rather than by consistent estimation of real value." And: "We need to know if the value investors have imputed to the market is not really there, so that we can adjust our planning and thinking. But a bubble is only discernible as such once most investors have ceased to put their money on those 'overvalued' stocks—in other words, once it is perceived to have popped." As this volume goes to press, the U.S. is at the end of another such cycle, this time involving the housing market: a bubble, again, defined as such only after it can be said to have popped. My subject is the way stock-market culture reads prices as reflections of human emotions, at the same time attaching human emotions to the supposed reality of stock prices. Such events as "booms" are, in this scenario, relatively short-lived bursts of feeling in the context of a longer emotional narrative: episodes whose boundaries come into view only when prices are generally perceived to have become less "rational" than usual. I agree with Peter Garber's view that "'[b]ubble' characterizations . . . are non-explanations of events, merely a name that we attach to a financial phenomenon that we have not invested sufficiently in understanding" (Shiller xii; Garber 124).

2. Contemporary examples include such figures as Ivan Boesky, Michael Milken, Martin Frankel and Jonathan Lebed, the last discussed in more detail below. Frankel's story is one of familial corruption and sexual debauchery as well as (the always-cited) greed; Boesky notoriously expressed the extent of his corruption when he commented—at a commencement address, no less—that "Greed is all right." When Lebed's case came to light, his relationship with his family was of much interest to reporters. In such cases, the Securities Exchange Commission appears (understandably) hapless, its job to regulate an institution antithetical to regulation.

3. While my leap from CNBC to Trollope may seem a long one, there is much to connect the economic climate of the late nineteenth century to that of the late twentieth and early twenty-first, most tellingly for my purposes widespread interest in and excitement about the movement of stock prices or, later, housing prices, and widespread participation in and identification with investments that become increasingly difficult to distinguish from speculations. Comments about the cross-class nature of investment, to the effect that "everyone is in it," appear in both periods; so too does a lengthening of the trading day, with its logical conclusion the phenomenon of 24/7 trading. Also similar is the promise that the new technologies largely responsible for excitement about the market (the railway, the internet) will transform society beyond recognition. In both periods, new technologies rely on a similarly fantasmatic relation between investor and objects of investment; in both, the activity of investment often takes place with little or no knowledge, on the investor's part, of what is being invested in. And both periods, of course, tie investment and speculation to character and feeling.

4. "The lower half of his face" may refer to the absence of a beard; in the novel, the phrase is never explained.

5. Trollope uses the term "admitted" similarly in relation to Augustus Melmotte: "Mr. Melmotte was admitted into society because of some enormous power that was supposed to be in his hands: but even by those who thus admitted him he was regarded as a thief and a scoundrel." (*The Way We Live Now* 247). On Britain's exportation of raw materials and goods and importation of manufactured goods from the mid 1870's on, see Checkland 62–64.

6. The suggestion is that Lopez's open admission of his foreignness might deflect Wharton's attention away from other, still-unspecified problems: "by admitting that openly he thought he might prevent discussion on matters which might, perhaps, be more disagreeable, but to which he need not allude if the accident of his birth were to be taken by the father as settling the question" (32). We are not told what these matters are: Lopez's financial activities and his Jewishness are, the implication is, equally and interchangeably disagreeable.

7. Thus while the definition of speculation is unstable, the insistence on a distinction between legitimate and illegitimate modes of investment is not. That stock-market discourse continues to insist on this difference even as the meanings of the terms shift (what Lopez does is now called options trading, for instance, and there is nothing illegitimate about it) both reveals the continuing presence of the nineteenth century in the twenty-first and explains why it is so easy not to see it. Any number of contemporary figures called "successful investors" are also contemporary versions of Ferdinand Lopez: Jim Rogers, for instance, who claims to "bet" on "whole countries," has this to say: "the only thing better is finding a country everybody's bullish on and shorting it" (Train 3). There is Michael Milken, said to have considered finance an art-form, and Jonathan Lebed, discussed below—both of whose activities, while widely considered immoral, were completely legal. But perhaps the more salient point is that anyone involved in the market today is a Lopez figure in the sense that he or she is merely "backing" opinion; our own Lopez-like qualities are obscured, however, by the speculator/investor dramas played out in public. A good investment gone bad becomes a speculation, and the search for culprits begins.

8. "My hope to rise had always been built on writing novels, and at last by writing novels I have risen" (*An Autobiography* 169).

9. Trollope's attention to "the business of life" has been discussed by Phillip Collins, who notes that, when introducing a character, Trollope "specifies his or her income or capital" (297). But to say this much is only to suggest, as Trollope criticism typically does, that in his novels and in his life the author displays an amusing and eccentric—and thus wholly "Victorian"—obsession with financial detail.

10. Shiller notes that we are surrounded by stock-market stories, in which successful investing is presented "as a process of mastering one's own impulses" (49).

11. In *Little Dorrit*, speculation is a "fever" and an "infection." Dickens thus suggests that a speculator is an ordinary person with a disorder. Says Pancks of Clennam, "'It was my misfortune to lead him into a ruinous investment' (Mr. Pancks still clung to that word, and never said speculation" [538]). The figure of the investor reinforces the characteristic Victorian division between work and home, while the speculator's imagined constant attention to his money attests to the unsavory nature of someone who has no other, or "real," life. In this way, the speculator turns out to be a strangely unified figure, and Victorian discomfort about him suggests the undesirability of such unity in such representations of identity. For another example, see Jaffe, *Sympathy* ch. 2.

12. The same phenomenon is observable in Lopez's partner, Sexty Parker: "Whenever, therefore, a much-needed sum of money was produced, Sexty would become light-hearted, triumphant, and very sympathetic" (372).

13. "But as ideas of this nature crowded themselves into her mind she told

herself again and again that she had taken him for better and for worse. If the worse were already coming, she would still be true to her promise. 'You had better tell papa everything,' she said" (301).

14. Says Wharton's son Everett: "My father never in his life said anything to me of his own money affairs, though he says a great deal about mine. No man ever was closer than my father. But I believe that he could afford almost anything" (18); see also 220.

15. Wishes play a role in Wharton's thoughts about Lopez: "He thought it probable that the man might have an adequate income, and yet he did not wish to welcome him as a son-in-law. . . . As he looked at Lopez, he thought he detected Jewish signs, but he was afraid to make any allusion to religion, lest Lopez should declare that his ancestors had been noted as Christians since St. James first preached in the Peninsula" (32). Wharton wishes, that is, not to find out that Lopez is not Jewish, and Lopez's Jewishness cannot but appear as other than the fulfillment of his wish.

16. Here, from the dot-com crash of the late 1990s and early 2000s, are some examples of the wrong kind of stories: "The stock price of Emulex, a maker of computer networking equipment, plunged early yesterday after a false negative report about the company was circulated" (Berenson). Also relevant is the story of Jonathan Lebed, a New Jersey teenager who made his avid attention to the CNBC numbers pay off by "attend[ing] high school by day and, according to securities regulators, manipulat[ing] stocks by night on his computer. When he was apprehended for his scheme of promoting obscure stocks on the Internet that he had recently bought himself, then selling the shares at higher prices to those who inexplicably acted on his anonymous tips, his response was 'Everybody does it.' In a world where analysts put outlandish price targets on stocks and money managers regularly promote the stocks they hold on CNBC, truer words were never spoken" (Morgenson). (This article hands out the annual "Augustus Melmotte Memorial Prize"—Lebed won for 2000.) The false report works, of course, because it looks exactly like a true one, and the "hair-trigger" state of the market reflects investors' awareness of their inability to tell the difference. A profile of Lebed by Michael Lewis makes a number of relevant points, including the idea that the Securities Exchange Commission was created because, "To the greater public in 1934, the numbers on the stock-market ticker no longer seemed to represent anything 'real,' but rather the result of manipulation by financial pros. So, how to make the market seem 'real'? The answer was to make new stringent laws against stock-market manipulation, whose job it was to make sure their machinations did not ever again unnerve the great sweaty rabble. That's not how the S.E.C. put it, of course" ("Extracurricular Activities" 32–33).

17. The numbers: from the bathroom scale to the SATs to the EKG to the NASDAQ. The stock market is tracked, it is perhaps needless to point out, by investors and noninvestors alike: "I am not a broker, a financial adviser, or even a day trader. Heck, I don't even own a single share of stock outright. So why can't I stop watching CNBC?" (Martin). Martin's use of the term "outright" is suggestive in light of *The Prime Minister*'s take on the need to keep one's distance from actual money: she implies that she owns stock, but only in some unspecified, indirect way, and at the same time reveals her vicarious involvement in the drama of what she permits herself to think of only as other peoples' money.

CHAPTER FOUR

1. For another reading of this bliss, see Miller. These moments and others like them have been discussed in numerous critical works, including my own *Vanishing Points* 112–28; Lougy 72–101; Westburg; Gilmour; and Bodenheimer 215–33.

2. Soni articulates something of the blankness of this term—the way repetition contributes to its apparent resistance to historical inquiry: "Insofar as there is no concept of happiness, only the immediate abstraction of an affect which simply says "I am happy" without further elaboration or qualification, there can be no history of the concept or its changes. . . . " The 'I am happy,'" he notes, "resembles nothing so much as the staccato repetition of the contentless 'It is beautiful' in a Kantian aesthetic judgment" (8). Gallagher takes up the issue of happiness in chapter 3 of *The Body Economic;* her discussion of Dickens's *Hard Times* addresses Dickens's satire of Bentham and insistent correlation of labor with unhappiness. Her argument supports an idea others have put forward about the absence of visible labor in *David Copperfield;* namely, that Dickens is "suspended . . . between wanting to acknowledge the importance of happiness and being unable to imagine how it might proceed from work" (82).

3. "For example, a typical self-rating question asks people to respond on a five-point scale to the question, 'Taking the good with the bad, how happy and contented are you on the average now, compared with other people?'" (Sugden, 92). The idea of measuring happiness may trace its history to what Baudrillard has described as a society's need, in the context of the idea of the rights of man, to offer "observable proof," as Jonathan Crary puts it, that "happiness and equality had in fact been attained." Writes Crary, "Happiness had to be 'measurable in terms of objects and signs'" (Jean Baudrillard, *La société de consommation,* cited by Crary 11). For a recent survey of the field, see Bruni and Porta. For another discussion of sociological surveys in the interest of constructing averages, see Igo, *Averaged American.*

4. Martha Nussbaum argues that *Hard Times* presents a modified utilitarianism, comparable to a social policy that seeks "to ask how well people are doing by asking how well their form of life has enabled them to function in a variety of distinct areas, including, but not limited to, mobility, health, education, political participation, and social relations. This approach refuses to come up with a single number, reducing quality to quantity" (*Poetic Justice* 51).

5. Darrin McMahon and others have discussed connections between debates about happiness and the growth of consumer society in the eighteenth century. McMahon writes, "in the 1700's the growth of urban centers was already creating new concentrated markets that served as a catalyst for what historians describe as the 'birth of consumer society.' By the mid-eighteenth century, a 'favorable conjuncture' of an expanding population and rising agricultural prices, coupled with a greater availability of credit and a massive boom in foreign trade, was paying dividends in the form of increased investment and sustained economic growth . . . luxuries were at hand and available to ever wider segments of the population . . . They appealed directly to the century's fascination with pleasure" (206).

6. See Gallagher's discussion, Introduction, note 24.

7. Janice Carlisle reads this passage as expressing a tension between activity

and passivity in Mill's character: "Mill imagines a kind of magical and instantaneous transformation during which all his goals as a 'reformer of the world' would be accomplished. What is missing from this vision of a dream achieved is his active role in its achievement. Like his position in the India House, this vision of fulfillment puts him on the sidelines. . . . He can find no personal happiness in a world not needing improvement because he sees no role for himself there . . . " (66). Her interpretation suggests, interestingly, that Mill wants to see himself not as an investor or a speculator, but as a worker. Barbara Gelpi has argued that Dickens's influence led Mill, Ruskin, and Pater to represent themselves in their autobiographies as Dickensian "waifs."

8. A. W. Levi supports the general idea that Mill's response to Marmontel is an "abreaction," allowing the discharge of repressed feeling. William Thomas argues against the idea that Mill did not fully understand his own experience, as most analyses suggest, proposing instead that he uses his associationist training to restore himself. And Nussbaum claims that rather than identifying with "bereaved Marmontel," as most critics suggest, Mill actually identified with "the orphaned family who were now going to receive the care they needed" (*Hiding* 190).

9. As in the case of the fruit beckoning in the window in "A Christmas Carol," a crucial aspect of Dickens's appeal was his ability to link the average with the ideal: to represent as acutely desirable goals that were potentially within everyone's grasp, such as a family or a Christmas dinner.

10. See the introduction for Soni's work on the changing nature of happiness in the eighteenth century.

11. I discuss this structure of recognition in Dickens's "A Christmas Carol" and in Wilde's *The Picture of Dorian Gray* in *Scenes of Sympathy*, 39–40 and 170–71. In order for Althusser's structure of ideological hailing (in which the subject turns in response to a policeman's call) to work, the subject must already identify with the authority or institution doing the hailing.

12. I mean to suggest both an identification with particular representations—cultural images of happiness—and a fundamental vicariousness: an identification with representation itself.

13. Happiness economics seeks to measure happiness, not money—at least it claims to measure the two separately. But the insistent cultural association between happiness and money, and the very idea of happiness as something to be measured, imagines the two not simply as related (as in, if you have one you probably have some of the other) but also as similar, susceptible to the same kind of analysis.

14. It is not surprising that happiness, defined either as like money or as separate from but equal to it, should be caught up in that structure of invidious distinctions known as the Victorian novel. For what is this novel in particular, and the Victorian novel in general, but a structure of invidious distinctions, in which the purpose of "subplots"—an invidious distinction if ever there was one—is to underscore the extent to which "central" characters have arrived at the best possible end: an end that never recommends the greatest happiness for the greatest number, but always the greatest happiness for only a few?

15. As Bodenheimer notes, in an interpretation that offers a counterpoint to my discussion of David in Steerforth's room, "In chapter 25 David unwillingly invites Uriah into his rooms, his bed, and his nightmares" (232). In a reading that empha-

sizes the characters' mutual vicariousness, Bodenheimer sees Uriah as pushing the limits of David's genteel code of enforced politeness.

16. "The Dickensian hero . . . enters a household that displaces any semblance of the complex and fraught social world he has successfully negotiated. At this point, the limits that the novel has set on his happiness miraculously vanish, along with the fact that such happiness is an exception to the social rule" (Armstrong, *How Novels Think* 144).

CONCLUSION

1. The initial data are unavailable for critique. Without subjecting any of these projects ("McBurney, Beasley, Raven, Garside and Block for Britain; Angus, Mylne and Frautschi for France . . . " [4]) to analysis, Moretti claims them as parts of a cooperative project from which independent facts can be extracted.

WORKS CITED

Ahmed, Sarah. *The Cultural Politics of Emotion*. New York: Routledge, 2004.

Alborn, Timothy. "Normal Bodies, Normal Prices: Interdisciplinarity in Victorian Life Insurance." *Ravon (Romanticism and Victorianism on the Net)* 48 (2008).

American Funds Investor (Fall–Winter 2001).

Anderson, Benedict. *Imagined Communities: Reflections on the Origin and Spread of Nationalism*. New York: Verso, 1983.

Armstrong, Nancy. *Fiction in the Age of Photography: The Legacy of British Realism*. Cambridge: Harvard University Press, 1999.

———. *How Novels Think: The Limits of Individualism from 1719–1900*. New York: Columbia University Press, 2005.

Bedient, Calvin. *Architects of the Self: George Eliot, D.H. Lawrence, and E.M. Forster*. Berkeley: University of California Press, 1972.

Berenson, Alex. "On Hair-Trigger Wall Street, a Stock Plunges on Fake News." *The New York Times*, August 26, 2000. 1:1.

Bernstein, Jake. *The Compleat Day Trader II*. New York: McGraw Hill, 1998.

Bodenheimer, Rosemarie. "Knowing and Telling in Dickens's Retrospects." In Suzy Anger, ed., *Knowing the Past: Victorian Literature and Culture*. Ithaca: Cornell University Press, 2001. 215–33.

Brennan, Teresa. *The Transmission of Affect*. Ithaca: Cornell University Press, 2004.

Buck-Morss, Susan. "Envisioning Capital: Political Economy on Display." In Peter Wollen, ed. *Visual Display*. New York: New Press, 1999.

Bulkowski, Thomas N. *Encyclopedia of Chart Patterns*. New York: Wiley and Sons, 2000.

Canguilhem, Georges. *The Normal and the Pathological*. New York: Zone Books, 1989.

Carret, Phillip L. *The Art of Speculation*. New York: Wiley and Sons, 1997.

Carlisle, Janice. *John Stuart Mill and the Writing of Character*. Athens: University of Georgia Press, 1991.

Castle, Terry. *The Female Thermometer: Eighteenth-Century Culture and the Invention of the Uncanny*. New York: Oxford University Press, 1995.

Checkland, S. G. *The Rise of Industrial Society in England, 1815–1885*. New York: St. Martin's Press, 1965.

Cohen, Patricia. "When Dockets Imitate Drama." *The New York Times,* December 27, 2008. C1: 10.

Collins, Phillip. "Business and Bosoms: Some Trollopian Concerns." *Nineteenth-Century Fiction* 37 (1982).

Cottom, Daniel. *Social Figures: George Eliot, Social History, and Literary Representation.* Minneapolis: University of Minnesota Press, 1987.

Crary, Jonathan. *Techniques of the Observer: On Vision and Modernity in the Nineteenth Century.* Cambridge, MA: MIT Press, 1990.

Cvetkovich, Ann. *Mixed Feelings: Feminism, Mass Culture, and Sensationalism.* New Brunswick: Rutgers University Press, 1992.

Desrosières, Alan. *The Politics of Large Numbers,* trans. Camille Nash. Cambridge: Harvard University Press, 1998.

Dickens, Charles. *David Copperfield.* Jeremy Tambling, ed. London: Penguin, 2004.

———. *Little Dorrit.* Harvey Peter Sucksmith, ed. Oxford: Oxford University Press, 1987.

Duncan, William Wallace. *Duncan on Investment in Stocks and Shares.* 2nd ed. London, 1894.

Eliot, George. *Middlemarch,* ed. W. J. Harvey. Harmondsworth. Penguin, 1965.

Ferguson, Frances. "Jane Austen, *Emma,* and the Impact of Form." *Modern Language Quarterly* 61 (2000).

Forster, John. *The Life of Charles Dickens.* London: Chapman and Hall, 1879.

Foucault, Michel. *The History of Sexuality.* Vol. 1: An Introduction, translated Robert Hurley. New York: Vintage, 1978.

———. *The Order of Things,* trans. Alan Sheridan. New York: Vintage, 1970.

Francis, John. *Chronicles and Characters of the Stock Exchange.* Boston: Wm. Crosby and H. P. Nichols, 1850.

Franzten, Jonathan. *The Corrections.* New York: Picador USA, 2001.

Freedman, Jonathan. *The Temple of Culture.* Oxford: Oxford University Press, 2000.

Gallagher, Catherine. *The Body Economic: Life, Death, and Sensation in Political Economy and the Victorian Novel.* Princeton: Princeton University Press, 2006.

———. "George Eliot: Immanent Victorian." *Proceedings of the British Academy* 94 (1996): 157–72.

Galton, Francis. *Natural Inheritance.* London: Macmillan, 1889.

Garber, Peter. *Famous First Bubbles: The Fundamentals of Early Manias.* Cambridge, MA: MIT Press, 2000.

Gelpi, Barbara. "The Innocent I: Dickens's Influence on Victorian Autobiography." In Jerome Buckley, ed., *The Worlds of Victorian Fiction.* Cambridge, MA: Harvard University Press, 1975. 57–71.

Gilmour, Robin. "Memory in *David Copperfield.*" *Dickensian* 71 (1975): 30–42.

Gore, Al. *An Inconvenient Truth.* Paramount Pictures, 2006.

Hacking, Ian. *The Taming of Chance.* Cambridge: Cambridge University Press, 1996.

Hennessy, Elizabeth. *Coffee House to Cyber Market: 200 Years of the London Stock Exchange.* London: Ebury Press, 2001.

Hochschild, Arlie Russell. *The Managed Heart: Commercialization of Human Feeling.* Berkeley: University of California, 1983.

Houston, Gail. *From Dickens to Dracula: Gothic, Economics, and Victorian Fiction.* Cambridge: Cambridge University Press, 2005.

Igo, Sarah. *The Averaged American: Surveys, Citizens, and the Making of a Mass Public.* Cambridge: Harvard University Press, 2007.

Jaffe, Audrey. *Scenes of Sympathy: Identity and Representation in Victorian Fiction.* Ithaca: Cornell University Press, 2000.

———. *Vanishing Points: Dickens, Narrative, and the Subject of Omniscience.* Berkeley: University of California Press, 1991.

Jevons, William Stanley. *A Theory of Political Economy.* London: Macmillan, 1876.

Kaplan, Cora. *Victoriana: History, Fictions, Criticism.* New York: Columbia University Press, 2008.

Klaver, Claudia. *A/Moral Economics: Classical Political Economy and Cultural Authority in Nineteenth-Century England.* Columbus: The Ohio State University Press, 2003.

Klein, Judy L. *Statistical Visions in Time: A History of Time Series Analysis, 1662–1938.* Cambridge: Cambridge University Press, 1997.

Krugman, Paul. "The Madoff Economy." *The New York Times,* December 19, 2008. A45.

Kucich, John, and Diane Sadoff, eds., *Victorian Afterlife: Postmodern Culture Rewrites the Nineteenth Century.* Minneapolis: University of Minnesota Press, 2000.

Lane, Christopher. *Shyness: How Normal Behavior Became a Sickness.* New Haven: Yale University Press, 2008.

Levi, A. W. "The Mental Crisis of John Stuart Mill." In John C. Wood, ed., *John Stuart Mill: Critical Assessments.* New York: Routledge, 1991. 124–36.

Lewis, Michael. "Jonathan Lebed's Extracurricular Activities." *The New York Times Magazine,* February 25, 2001.

———. *The Money Culture.* New York: Penguin, 1991.

Lewis, Michael J. "In a Changing Skyline, a Sudden, Glaring, Void." *The New York Times,* September 16, 2001. 4:4.

Lo, Andrew W., and Dmitry V. Repin. "The Psychophysiology of Real-Time Financial Risk Processing," *Journal of Cognitive Neuroscience* 14:3 (2002): 323–39.

Logan, Peter. *Nerves and Narratives: A Cultural History of Hysteria in 19th-Century British Prose.* Berkeley: University of California Press, 1997.

Lougy, Robert E. "Remembrances of Death Past and Future: A Reading of *David Copperfield.*" *Dickens Studies Annual* 6 (1977): 72–101.

Luigino, Bruni, and Pier Luigi Porta, eds. *Economics and Happiness: Framing the Analysis.* New York: Oxford, 2005.

Lynch, Deidre. *The Economy of Character: Novels, Market Culture, and the Business of Inner Meaning.* Chicago: University of Chicago Press, 1987.

Maas, Harro. "An Instrument Can Make a Science: Jevons's Balancing Act in Economics." In Judy L. Klein and Mary S. Morgan, eds., *The Age of Economic Measurement.* Durham: Duke University Press, 2001.

MacKay, Charles. *Extraordinary Popular Delusions and the Madness of Crowds.* Andrew Tobias, ed. New York: Three Rivers Press, 1980.

Martin, Linda Carroll. "Live From New York, the Trading Day." *The New York Times,* July 9, 2000. C:7.

Mayhew, Henry. *London Labour and the London Poor.* Vol. III. New York: Dover, 1968.

McClintock, Anne. *Imperial Leather: Race, Gender, and Sexuality in the Colonial Context.* New York: Routledge, 1995.

McCullagh, Declan. "Database Nation." *Reason*, June 2004. www.reason.com/news/show/29148.html

McMahon, Darrin. *A History of Happiness*. New York: Atlantic Monthly Press, 2006.

Michie, Ranald. *The London Stock Exchange: A History*. Oxford: Oxford University Press, 1999.

Mill, John Stuart. *Autobiography*. Indianapolis: Bobbs-Merril, 1957.

Miller, D. A. *The Novel and the Police*. Berkeley: University of California Press, 1988.

Morgan, Mary S. "Making Measuring Instruments." In Judy L. Klein and Mary Morgan, eds., *The Age of Economic Measurement*. Durham: Duke University Press, 2001. 242–43.

Moretti, Franco. *Graphs, Maps, and Trees*. New York: Verso, 2003.

Morgenson, Gretchen. "Market Watch." *The New York Times*, December 31, 2000. 3:9.

Morris, Pam. *Imagining Inclusive Society in Nineteenth-Century Novels*. Baltimore: Johns Hopkins University Press, 2004.

Mottram, R. H. *A History of Financial Speculation*. Boston: Little, 1929.

Mukerjee, Amitabha. "The Mathematics of Happiness." *Storytelling Science*. www.cse.iitk.ac.in~amit/story/12_math-happiness.html.

Nissenblatt, Michael, M.D. Letter, *The New York Times Magazine*, December 2, 2001. 26.

Nussbaum, Martha. *Hiding from Humanity: Disgust, Shame, and the Law*. Princeton: Princeton University Press, 2004.

———. *Poetic Justice: The Literary Imagination and Public Life*. Boston: Beacon Press, 1995.

Pinch, Adela. *Strange Fits of Passion: Epistemologies of Emotion, Hume to Austen*. Stanford: Stanford University Press, 1994.

Plotz, John. *The Crowd: British Literature and Public Politics*. Berkeley: University of California Press, 2000.

Poovey, Mary. *The Financial System in Victorian Britain*. New York: Oxford University Press, 2003.

———. *A History of the Modern Fact*. Chicago: University of Chicago, 1998.

———. *Making a Social Body: British Cultural Formation, 1830–1864*. Chicago: University of Chicago Press, 1995.

———. "The Structure of Anxiety in Political Economy and *Hard Times*." In Suzy Anger, ed., *Knowing the Past: Victorian Literature and Culture*. Ithaca: Cornell University Press, 2001.

Porter, Theodore. *The Rise of Statistical Thinking, 1820–1900*. Princeton: Princeton University Press, 1986.

———. *Trust in Numbers*. Princeton: Princeton University Press, 1995.

Quetelet, Adolphe. *Treatise on Man*. Edinburgh: W. R. Chambers, 1842.

Reed, John. "A Friend to Mammon: Speculation in Victorian Literature." *Victorian Studies* 27 (1984): 179–202.

Rosmarin, Adena. *The Power of Genre*. Minneapolis: University of Minnesota Press, 1985.

Schabas, Margaret. *A World Ruled by Number: William Stanley Jevons and the Rise of Mathematical Economics*. Princeton: Princeton University Press, 1990.

Schor, Juliet. *The Overspent American: Why We Want What We Don't Need*. New York: Harper Perennial, 1985.

Schott, John W. *Mind over Money.* Boston: Little, Brown, 1998.

Sedgwick, Eve. *Touching Feeling: Affect, Pedagogy, Performativity.* Durham: Duke University Press, 2004.

Sekula, Alan. "The Body and the Archive." *October* 39 (1986): 3–64.

Seltzer, Mark. *Serial Killers: Death and Life in America's Wound Culture.* New York: Routledge, 1998.

Shiller, Robert. *Irrational Exuberance.* Princeton: Princeton University Press, 2000.

Shuman, Cathy. *Pedagogical Economies: The Examination and the Victorian Literary Man.* Stanford: Stanford University Press, 2000.

Silverman, Kaja. *Male Subjectivity at the Margins.* New York: Routledge, 1992.

Simmel, Georg. *On Individuality and Social Forms.* Chicago: University of Chicago, 1972.

Soni, Visvathan. "Affecting Happiness: The Emergence of the Modern Political Subject in the Eighteenth Century." Dissertation Duke University, 2000.

Stein, Rob. "Hormones Tied to Traders' Deal-Making, Study Finds." http://www.washingtonpost.com, April 21, 2008.

Stigler, Steven. *The History of Statistics: The Measurement of Uncertainty before 1900.* Cambridge: Harvard University Press, 1986.

Sugden, Robert. "Correspondence of Sentiments: An Explanation of the Pleasure of Social Interaction." In Luigino Bruni and Pier Luigi Porta, eds., *Economics and Happiness: Framing the Analysis.* New York: Oxford, 2005.

Terada, Rei. *Feeling in Theory: Emotion after "The Death of the Subject."* Cambridge: Harvard University Press, 2001.

Thomas, William. "John Stuart Mill and the Uses of Autobiography." In G. W. Smith, ed., *John Stuart Mill's Social and Political Thought.* New York: Routledge, 1998. 171–92.

Train, John. *The New Money Masters: Winning Investment Strategies of Soros, Lynch, Steinhardt, Rogers, Neff, Wanger, Michaelis, Carret.* New York: Harper and Row, 1989.

Trollope, Anthony. *An Autobiography.* Michael Sadleir and Frederick Page, eds. Oxford: Oxford World's Classics, 1992.

———. *The Prime Minister,* ed. David Skilton. Harmondsworth: Penguin, 1994.

———. *The Way We Live Now,* ed. Frank Kermode. Harmondsworth: Penguin, 1994

Veblen, Thorstein. *The Theory of the Leisure Class.* New York: Dover, 1994.

Westburg, Barry. *The Confessional Fictions of Charles Dickens.* De Kalb: Northern Illinois University Press, 1977.

Williams, Carolyn. "Moving Pictures: George Eliot and Melodrama." In Lauren Berlant, ed., *Compassion: The Culture and Politics of an Emotion.* New York: Routledge, 2004. 105–44.

Woloch, Alex. *The One vs. the Many: Minor Characters and the Space of the Protagonist in the Nineteenth-Century Novel.* Princeton: Princeton University Press, 2003.

Woodmansee, Martha, and Mark Osteen, eds., *The New Economic Criticism: Studies at the Intersection of Literature and Economics.* New York: Routledge, 1999.

Wright, Robert E. ed. *The History of Corporate Finance.* London: Pickering & Chatto, 2003.

Ziegler, Garrett. "The City of London, Real and Unreal." *Victorian Studies* 49 (2007): 431–55.

Ahmed, Sarah, 17, 116n7, 121n2
Alborn, Timothy, 113
Althusser, Louis, 12, 89, 115n5, 117n11, 120n8, 127n11
Anderson, Benedict ,118n19
Armstrong, Nancy, 3, 9, 115n6, 116n8, 116n9, 117n16
Autobiography (John Stuart Mill), 17, 21, 81–83, 86–101, 127n7, 127n8
An Autobiography (Anthony Trollope), 71
average, 5, 8, 17, 19–20, 43, 116n6, 118n18, 120n8; as abstraction, 5; defined, 9–14, 111–12; happiness, 16, 823; heartbeat, 34, 117n13; idealized, 17, 40, 127n9; mathematical definition of, 6, 117n3; in medicine, 121n16, 122n8. *See also* average man
average man, 3–4, 14, 16, 20–21, 22, 90, 111, 119n4, 119n6, 122n7; in *Middlemarch*, 23–41; trader as, 62; voter as, 112

Bagehot, Walter, 118n19
Barthes, Roland, 94
Baudrillard, Jean, 126n3
Bedient, Calvin, 25–26, 12n12
Bentham, Jeremy, 11, 18, 36, 86, 98, 119n24, 126n2; felicific calculus 16, 36–37, 98

Bertillon, Alphonse, 9–15, 19, 117n14
Bloom, Harold, 110
Bodenheimer, Rosemarie, 126n1, 127n15
Braudel, Fernand, 104
Bruni, Luigino, 126n3
Buck-Morss, Susan, 117n12

Canguilhem, Georges, 102, 116n10, 117n13, 118 n18, 121n16
Carlisle, Janice, 126n7
capitalism, 3, 59, 80, 119n25
Caplan, Cora, 114
Carret, Philip, 42, 64
Castaing, John, 53
Castle, Terry, 4, 9, 93, 111, 122n8
Cohen, Patricia, 118
Collins, Phillip, 124n9
consumption, 11, 67, 127n19
Cottom, Daniel, 119n1
The Corrections (Jonathan Frantzen), 21
Crary, Jonathan, 117n12, 126n3
Cvetkovich, Ann 47, 122n4

David Copperfield (Charles Dickens), 3, 8, 17, 21, 81–101, 126n2
Desrosières, Alain, 4–8, 20, 24–28, 102, 116n10, 119n2, 119n3, 119n7, 120n11

Dickens, Charles, 17, 20–21, 55, 58, 81–83, 87, 89–90, 99–101, 124n11, 127n7, 127n9, 127n11, 128n16. See also *David Copperfield; Little Dorrit*
distant reading, 7, 12, 14, 19, 46, 82, 86–89, 90, 102–114

Eliot, George, 8, 23–31, 33–34, 36–39, 40, 90, 119n1, 120n12, 121n17. See also *Middlemarch*
emotion: average, 25; and character, 27; collective, 2, 6, 19, 22, 84; as cultural product, 14; individual, 2, 7, 19, 116n9, 119n23; investment of, 6, 112; and money, 3, 18; quantification of, 17. *See also* exuberance; feeling; happiness
exuberance: irrational, 20, 65–66, 76, 79, 80, 83; rational, 80

feeling: and affect/emotion, 16–17; as bubble, 75; collective, 2–3, 19–20; gentlemanly, 70–72; and the Jew, 78–79; measurement of, 11; and money, 68, 71, 74, 79; objectification of, 17, 39; stock market, and 65–66. *See also* emotion; exuberance; happiness
Ferguson, Frances, 116n8
Foucault, Michel, 8, 107
Francis, John, 47–49, 51, 54, 57–58
Frantzen, Jonathan: *The Corrections*, 21
Freedman, Jonathan, 122n8
furniture: bad, 33–36, 39–40, 94, 98

Gallagher, Catherine, 3, 5–6, 115n4, 119n3, 119n24, 122n1, 126n2
Galton, Francis, 1–2, 5, 8, 10, 12, 14–16, 19, 103, 109, 115n1
Garber, Peter, 123n1
Gelpi, Barbara, 127n7
genre: concept of, 107–8, 110; and generation, 105–6, 109
gentleman, 32; in Trollope, 67–68, 70–72, 74, 77–79

Gilmour, Robin, 126n1
Gore, Al, 111–12
graph: bell curve, 14, 26; emotions, 37; as novel, 111; Moretti's, 102–14; and skyline, 59; stock-market, 14–19, 43, 47, 64, 72, 74, 77–78

Hacking, Ian, 120n11
happiness, 3, 7–10, 13, 15–28, 89; average, 82; as currency, 85–86; economics, 17–18, 83–85, 87–90, 97; and measurement, 16, 40, 65, 73, 75, 82, 97; in *David Copperfield*, 81–101; in Mill, 81, 86–89
Hayek, Friedrich, 122n8
Hennessy, Elizabeth, 48, 53
Hochschild, Arlie Russell, 121n2
Houston, Gail Turley, 115n4, 118n19

ideology, 4, 19–21, 62, 89, 113; domestic, 82, 98, 100; and happiness, 81
identity: collective, 2, 35–36, 38, 113; individual, 2, 5–7, 29–30, 36, 38, 116n9; middle-class, 21, 94, 117n11, 118n20, 120n8, 124n11
Igo, Sarah, 116n6, 126n3
An Inconvenient Truth (Al Gore), 111–12
investor, 8, 19–20, 42–47, 51–52, 54–56, 58–59, 65, 69, 72–74, 76, 87, 111–12, 124n11, 125n16, 125n17, 123n3, 124n7, 127n7. *See also* speculator

Jaffe, Audrey, 124n11
Jew, 66–67, 76–77, 124n6, 125n15; as speculator, 77–79
Jevons, William Stanley, 11–14, 27, 36–40, 121n18

Klaver, Claudia, 115n4
Klein, Judy L., 25, 102, 116n10
Krugman, Paul, 118
Kucich, John, 119n25

Lacan, Jacques, 10, 117n16
Lane, Christopher, 113
Lebed, Jonathan, 123n2, 124n7,
   125n16
Levi, A. W., 127n8
Lewis, Michael, 125n16
Lewis, Michael J., 59
Little Dorrit (Charles Dickens), 8,
   20–21, 46, 55, 58, 83, 124n11
Lougy, Robert, 126n1
Lynch, Deidre, 4, 119n1

Mackay, Charles, 52, 60
Madoff, Bernard, 118
Manheim, Karl, 106, 109
Marmontel, Jean-François, *Mémoires:*
   88–90, 97, 101, 127n8
Mayhew, Henry: *London Labour and
   the London Poor,* 28–29, 120n9
McClintock, Anne, 115n6
McCullagh, Declan, 120n15
McMahon, Darrin, 15, 126n5
Michie, Ranald, 48–50, 53, 57, 122n5,
   122n6, 122n7
Mill, John Stuart, 17, 21, 81–83, 86–90,
   93, 99, 101, 127n7, 127n8. See also
   Autobiography
Middlemarch (George Eliot), 3, 8, 17–
   18, 21, 23–41, 83–44, 90, 119n1
Milken, Michael, 124n7
Mill, John Stuart, 17, 21, 81–83, 86–90,
   93, 99, 101, 127n7, 127n8. See also
   Autobiography
Miller, D. A., 126n1
Moretti, Franco, 6–7, 14, 22, 102–14
Morgenson, Gretchen, 125n16
Morris, Pam, 115n2
Mukerjee, Amitabha, 83

9/11, 59
Nussbaum, Martha, 126n4, 127n8

photography, 3, 10, 115n6, 117n12
Pinch, Adela, 4
Plotz, John, 116n9

Poovey, Mary, 2–3, 5–7, 45, 115n2,
   115n4, 116n10, 118n19, 119n2,
   121n2, 122n3
Porta, Pier Luigi, 126n3
Porter, Theodore, 10, 12–13, 28, 102,
   116n10, 118n17, 119n2
The Prime Minister (Anthony Trollope), 8, 20–21, 46, 56–80

quantification, 4–5, 9, 18–19, 25,
   83, 112, 115n6; of feeling, 83; of
   happiness, 83; money and, 18;
   nineteenth-century, 9, 18, 25, 112,
   115n6
Quetelet, Adolphe, 10–14, 19, 26–31,
   33, 37, 103, 109–10, 117n13,
   118n17, 118n18, 119n4, 119n6,
   120n13

Rancière, Jacques, 4, 19
Reed, John, 122n9
Rosmarin, Adena, 107

Sadoff, Diane, 119n25
Schor, Juliet, 84–85, 96
Schott, John, 43–44, 46, 73
Sedgwick, Eve Kosofsky, 16–17
Sekula, Alan, 117n4, 120n13
Seltzer, Mark, 116n9, 119n5
Shiller, Robert, 43, 122n1, 124n10
Shuman, Cathy, 115n6
Silverman, Kaja, 4, 115n5, 117n11
Simmel, Georg, 43
skyline, New York City, 59
Soni, Visvathan, 16–17, 118n22, 126n2,
   127n10
speculator, 8, 15, 20, 42, 45–46, 51, 54,
   56–57, 68–69, 71–8, 87, 111, 121n2,
   122n8, 124n7, 124n11, 127n7. *See
   also* investor
statistics, 1–2, 4, 7–8, 12, 26–31, 25, 38,
   57, 102, 104, 113, 118n17, 119n2,
   121n16
stock market: bubbles 59, 65, 73, 75,
   122n1; and character, 51–56; 58;

66–80; and the heart, 51–54, 59, 66; and feeling, 53–55; 65–80; as novel, 56–58
Sturken, Marita, 111

Trollope, Anthony, 8, 20, 63, 65–66, 68, 71–72, 76, 78–79, 87, 99, 123n3, 123n5, 124n9. See also *An Autobiography; The Prime Minister*

Veblen, Thorstein, 84–85, 87, 97, 99–100

weather: internal, 93, 111
Westburg, Barry, 126n4
Woloch, Alex, 29, 119n1

Zeigler, Garrett, 122n7

VICTORIAN CRITICAL INTERVENTIONS
Donald E. Hall, Series Editor

Included in this series are provocative, theory-based forays into some of the most heated discussions in Victorian studies today, with the goal of redefining what we both know and do in this field.

Lost Causes: Historical Consciousness in Victorian Literature
Jason B. Jones

Problem Novels: Victorian Fiction Theorizes the Sensational Self
Anna Maria Jones

Detecting the Nation: Fictions of
Detection and the Imperial Venture
Caroline Reitz

Novel Professions: Interested Disinterest and the Making
of the Professional in the Victorian Novel
Jennifer Ruth

Perspectives: Modes of Viewing and Knowing
in Nineteenth-Century England
Linda M. Shires

Performing the Victorian: John Ruskin and Identity in Theater,
Science, and Education
Sharon Aronosky Weltman

The Old Story, with a Difference: Pickwick's Vision
Julian Wolfreys